# The
# Pastor's Problems

# The
# Pastor's Problems

EDITED BY

CYRIL S. RODD

T. & T. CLARK LIMITED
36 GEORGE STREET, EDINBURGH

Copyright © T. & T. Clark Limited, 1985

Typeset by Blackwood Pillans & Wilson, Edinburgh,
printed and bound by Page Brothers (Norwich) Limited,

for

T. & T. CLARK LIMITED, EDINBURGH

First printed 1985

British Library Cataloguing in Publication Data
Rodd, Cyril S.
    The Pastor's Problems.
    1. Clergy—Office
    I. Title
    262'.14      BV660.2

ISBN 0 567 29117 0

# Contents

98168

# Preface

THIS book originated in a series of articles in *The Expository Times*. When I began the series I did not foresee that it would run for nearly four years and that when I decided to bring it to an end readers would still be suggesting further topics that needed discussion. Clearly it fulfilled a need.

The aim was strictly practical. As I wrote to the first contributors: 'The title is alliterative, but the intention is not to analyse the problems but to offer severely practical advice and help to ministers and clergy who are struggling'. I was looking for positive suggestions, and I wanted to get them from priests and ministers who were actually doing the job. Most of the contributors do fall into this category, although some moved to administrative and other posts after the articles had been agreed.

In planning the series I had three groups of ministers chiefly in mind. First there were those who had grown stale. The round of church activities had become a routine. They were over-faced by the task of just keeping the church going. Then there were younger clergy who were having difficulty in finding their feet. Missing the fellowship and corporate devotional life of college, and discovering that they were expected to play the part of the minister on all occasions whatever their own private feelings, they could all too easily become professionals in the bad sense of the term, or their sense of vocation might falter. Finally there were ordinands; and I thought not only of the younger men and women in theological colleges but also, and perhaps more especially, of those who had entered upon ordination courses after a long period of secular work, some to become non-stipendiary ministers.

The articles fall into five sections, with an introductory discussion of 'The Pastor's Priorities'.

No one can introduce others to God unless he lives close to God himself. So the first section concerns the pastor's own religious life of prayer, study and Bible-reading.

We then turn to the pastor's more 'churchly' activities — worship, sermon-writing and the main *rites de passage*.

Although the title 'Pastor' was chosen for the alliteration, the term is a reminder of the minister's duty to care for the people under his charge. The third section deals with visiting in general and visiting the sick and the dying in particular, with one further issue that has come to the fore in recent years, meeting the young fundamentalist.

But the pastor's life includes the common round, and the next group of contributors consider four aspects of this — the pastor's own family, his relations with colleagues, money matters and administration.

Finally two articles look more broadly at training, with special reference to continuing training throughout the pastor's whole ministry and assessing his work.

Readers will readily think of other topics that should have been included, and a number were suggested to me — communication within the parish (and running a parish magazine), contact with outsiders, leading groups of various kinds, coping in crisis, youth work, the pastor and the Sunday School or Junior Church, ecumenical relations at the local level and many more. Certainly more articles on pastoral care were needed and this is being met in a series in *The Expository Times*, 'First Aid in Pastoral Care', which will also be issued as a book. The reasons for the omission of particular topics were various. Once or twice a prospective contributor dashed the suggestion, as when I wrote to a distinguished minister with a request for an article on 'The Woman Minister'. The minister replied that she did not think of herself as a 'woman minister' (did I think of myself as a 'man minister') and in any case she could think of no problems specific to women ministers. Sometimes my contacts were not adequate to secure suitable writers. One contributor died.

The length of the articles inevitably means that none of the 'problems' has been dealt with in depth. I think, however, that what is lost in the brevity has to some extent been compensated by the directness with which all the contributors write. All made determined efforts to keep to their brief. It seems to me that what the clergy to whom the series was addressed needed was primarily encouragement and fresh ideas. The contributors provide this. They also offer the support of men and women who write from a firmly grounded spirituality and who have thought their way through theologically.

Finally I must express my appreciation to the contributors, who responded so readily and enthusiastically to my requests, and to those readers who took the trouble to write to me with comments, criticisms, and, most of all, extremely helpful suggestions.

CYRIL S. RODD

# Introduction

# The Pastor's Priorities

### J. DAVID BRIDGE, B.A., B.D.
London

ANYONE who observes the life of a minister in pastoral work must be struck immediately by two paradoxes. The first is that while there can be few occupations in which a person is as free to decide what to do and when to do it, the constant complaint is of being trapped in a web of obligations from which there is apparently no escape. The second is that while the ministry is clearly one of the 'helping' professions the minister receives so little help. Taken together these two point to what might be called without exaggeration the greatest need of the ministry today which is the ability to cope with freedom. Where we cannot cope, when we lose our grip on right priorities, the whole of our ministry is undermined. The gifts we bring to our work cannot be deployed while the grace which should suffuse our task is overwhelmed by frustration and ultimately by cynicism and despair. This is why, of all the tasks facing the ordained ministry today, none is more important than the discovery and sustaining of priorities which reflect the gospel we proclaim.

Freedom and flexibility are inherent in the pastoral ministry as we know it. No minister works set hours, refusing to talk to someone who seeks help at 5.35 p.m. or ignoring the telephone because it happens to be Monday. Our calling is to be available to people in their need. Being available to people in their need is not, however, the same as being at people's beck and call. Our freedom carries with it the obligation to evaluate the appeals for help that come to us. Unless we say no to some we shall soon be in the position of being unable to say yes to any. Nor can we pass to others the responsibility for making judgments of this kind. I have been most fortunate in recent years in having church stewards with a deep concern for the pastoral care of the ministry. Dialogue with them was an essential part of the process whereby decisions about priorities were reached, but they could not make the decisions for me. No one knew the people, the church, or my own limitations as well as I did. If the decisions proved mistaken I had to be answerable for them. The burden of freedom cannot be avoided or transferred. Our problems are further complicated by the difficulty of deciding when we are actually at work. If we go shopping and meet members of our church in the supermarket, is that a domestic or a pastoral occasion? If I read the newspaper am I simply relaxing or storing up themes for next Sunday's intercessions? These questions have no answer; they simply make the task of finding priorities that much harder.

Probing deeper into the nature of the problem we might set it out under three headings, conceptual, historical and perceptual. There is a conceptual problem summed up in the question, what is a minister. If our conception of what a minister is lacks clarity, it is not surprising if our understanding of what a minister should be doing is vague. I judge that we are moving out of a period in which the ministry suffered from an acute lack of confidence in its role. During this time ministers have sometimes sought to justify themselves in terms that would make sense to a secular public. Even if no one knew what a good minister was they would recognize a good social worker, a good teacher, or a good broadcaster. So priorities were taken over from other professions, and if this failed we could always fall back on the priority of hard work. Most people can be relied upon to appreciate hard work even if it is directed to no discernible end. The re-awakening of confidence in the ordained ministry as a profession in its own right is an important first step towards the establishing of ministerial priorities.

There is secondly an historical dimension to the problem which can be seen in two ways; we inherit a set of priorities when we move to a new appointment, and we bring our own models of ministry constructed out of past memories of other ministers. On the first Sunday in a new appointment, if not before, a minister will be made aware of a certain pattern of expectations; the minister's Friendly Hour always meets on a Wednesday; the Sewing Circle occupies the manse living room on a Friday, countless organizations expect the minister to address them at intervals throughout the season. It takes a particularly strong nerve to spurn the Friends and to cast out the embroiderers, but unless we do this we are in chains. Equally constricting is a personal model of ministry derived from rather impersonal contact with ministers in our adolescence. As a boy I formed a very clear impression of what a minister was. He was the person who gave an event significance. When he was not preaching the congregation was decimated. From the autumn play (which required a hymn and a prayer to precede it) to the AGM of the table tennis club the presence of the minister was *de rigueur*. Now the fact that a fringe member of the congregation believes in the indispensability of the ministry is of no consequence; it is when the ministers themselves start believing it that trouble starts. From then on it is not a question of priorities but of survival.

Thirdly there is the difficulty of perceiving the most urgent and pressing needs within a situation. When we have developed a working concept of what a minister is and freed ourselves from the millstone of faulty historical models the real task remains; how to interpret and evaluate the multitude of needs that press their claims upon us. In our preaching, how can we choose the themes that are related most closely to our people's needs? In our visiting, can we resist those who grumble most loudly about not seeing enough of the minister and seek out those who have a deep longing for a pastoral call but would never dream of mentioning this to a soul? In the planning of our diaries what proportion of time should be spent among Christians and what among unbelievers? In questions such as these are the real issues of a pastor's priorities rooted.

We may tackle them in three stages. The first is to set boundaries to our work time. This is the hardest step of all and many pastors will recoil from it. Yet without it there is no way in which we can begin to talk about priorities. Setting limits to the time we spend at work need not prevent us from being available to people in their need. No minister can or would want to exclude the possibility of leisure being interrupted by emergencies or unforeseen events. (Though we do need time which is free even from the possibility of interruption and must take care to arrange this also.) What we can do is to set limits to the time in which we are prepared to contemplate foreseen events. This will both enable us to feel positive towards leisure and will compel us to face the need to choose priorities. It will also enable us to have time for those we need most, our families and closest friends.

The second step is to examine our inability to say no. Is it because we feel indispensable? Have we overlooked the possibility that God has other resources for ministry? Have we forgotten that our ability to respond to the most important opportunities depends on our ability to decline the less important? If we refuse to make choices we become mere reflections of what others expect of us. Worse still, we are found to be unfaithful to the example of Jesus who sometimes found it necessary to withdraw from people in need in order to preserve the wholeness of his ministry, who found time to go to parties and to be alone and to walk in the countryside and who, to the great annoyance of some of his contemporaries, refused to copy John the Baptist's life of austerity, preferring to live it up with any who cared to call themselves his friends.

The effect of this should be to liberate us for the third task which is to make a personal inventory of the elements in ministry that matter to us most. If I offer my own it is not with the thought that this will necessarily be right for everyone. With God's help we must choose our own priorities. Nevertheless if what you find here commends itself to you, so be it.

I find that my priorities fall into two groups. This follows from what I understand a minister to be. A minister is what he is and what he does. (Forgive me if I do not constantly repeat he or she which becomes tedious.) What is special about a minister is not one particular characteristic or function but the combination of a number of characteristics and functions. More than in any other occupation a minister offers himself. You can act the clown without being a happy person, or direct social services without being a kind person, or teach ethics without being a good person, but you cannot be a minister without being a ministering person. Because no one enters the ministry with these gifts fully matured, the development of the gifts of ministry is as important a part of being a minister as the exercise of these gifts. Preparing ourselves to be ministers does not end at ordination; it is an integral part of our whole lives. So I need two general types of priority; those that help me to be equipped for the job to which I am called, and those that belong to the practice of my calling.

Being a minister involves me most of all in being four kinds of persons:

(i) One who prays. Like every Christian I need to receive what God through his Holy Spirit wishes to share with me. Through prayer I attune myself to what he is doing and seek to be a part of it. But the ordained ministry has two special characteristics with regard to prayer. Firstly we have more time for it than many people. Secondly it is our privilege to lead others in prayer in public worship. At the top of my list of priorities must come therefore time for prayer and time to cultivate a richer experience of prayer.

(ii) One who studies the faith. I must know what I believe and why. One of my early convictions which has not been modified during the years is that ignorance is a major obstacle to evangelism. The great majority of people in our country do not know what the Christian faith is about, though a number think they do and that makes matters worse. Few things therefore are more important than teaching in the life of the church. We must understand what the Christian faith is and on what foundations it rests, and be able to share with others both our insights and our desire to learn.

(iii) One who understands the world. If I am to help people who live in our society I must live in it myself and understand it. If I have a prophetic ministry I must know to what circumstances of life I am applying a Christian perspective. My preaching about dishonesty will carry more weight if I know what forms dishonesty takes in our society, and my pleading with a congregation to care for the poor will be so much futility (after all they already want to care for the poor) unless I can suggest ways in which the poor can be relieved of their distress. But my discovery of the nature of society must not merely be an academic exercise. If I have children I must learn through experience what it is to bring up a family in a Christian way or I cannot share these insights with others. If I do not give time to studying the world in which I live I risk making inoperative all other gifts of ministry.

(iv) One who communicates. The Christian faith is something to be shared. This sharing takes place through many channels and I am not going to be competent in more than one or two. Yet I must give time to this aspect of my development as a minister, how to be a better communicator. As I come to understand how prayer and the faith and our contemporary society belong together I must help others to make these discoveries for themselves. Being a Christian is not just a private mystery it involves a longing that all might have an experience of God through which they live in his world in the power of his Spirit.

Then there are four priorities which attach to the practice of ministry.

(v) Communicating. It is no accident that this ends my first group and begins my second. The two paragraphs could be merged together because often we learn best about communication when we are communicating. However, I leave them separate to emphasize that communication deserves priority both in our studying to be more effective ministers and in the deployment of our time as ministers. There are more forms of communication open to us than to our forebears and we have to decide which means are, for whatever reason, especially appropriate for ourselves. Some will find openings through local radio, others in a newspaper column. Some have musical, artistic, dramatic, or model-making gifts that will assist communication. All should be able to communicate through personal conversation though this is for many ministers the most difficult of all, gifts which have been developed for public meetings being not always suitable for private persons. I still rate preaching very highly as a means of communication. There are ministers who disparage preaching. I wonder if they know how many people come to worship longing to hear a good sermon.

(vi) Cultivating personal relationships. God is personal and while his Spirit works in many ways he often chooses to work through personal relationships. Nothing must be allowed to prevent us from spending a large part of every working week cultivating and developing relationships with people. This is what I understand to be the purpose of most pastoral visitations. There are those who will only visit in times of crisis or tragedy, but I believe they are gravely mistaken. This 'fire-brigade' approach to the pastoral ministry overlooks the fact that we can best help in a time of crisis those people with whom we have already built up a relationship of understanding and trust. Moreover the lack of personal contact with a congregation robs our preaching of a most important element, a truth to which I am able to bear especial testimony in my present role as a hit-and-run preacher. Nor should these personal relationships be confined to members of the church family. Equally important are regular contacts and sustained friendships with unbelievers.

(vii) Creating possibilities of worship. Just as the unique and supremely important task of the church is to give people opportunities for worship, so the role of the church's ministers must be to initiate and play a creative part in such worship. This does not always mean of course taking the lead in acts of worship. It certainly means involving others much more than has been customary in the past. But the responsibility for worship is ours and few things can be more important than this.

(viii) Releasing the gifts of the people of God. Throughout this article the word ministry has been used almost always in the sense of the ordained ministry. This was convenient, but it ought not to mislead us into thinking that ministry is exclusively the province of an ordained person. There is a ministry of the whole church and there is an urgent need for this ministry to be identified and released. The minister who does not recognize the limitations as well as the opportunities conferred by ordination and tries to do everything, far from increasing the total ministerial effort actually decreases it. When we have found time to communicate the faith, to relate to people as a minister of the church, and to create opportunities for people to worship, our next most urgent task is to discover and nurture the gifts of our people and to enable them to be exercised in ministry.

These are my eight priorities. Some will want to add to them and some will find them too many. They are as much as I can cope with and yet to lose any would be to undermine the rest. What is the point of understanding the faith if I cannot communicate it? What value is an understanding of the world if I do not know any people in the world? How can I pray yet not want to help others discover how to be open to the Spirit of God?

So to a brief practical postscript; how are these aims to be realized? I have said we cannot pass to others the responsibility for choosing priorities and this is true. It is equally true that we need others to help us in the never-ending task of perceiving and holding on to the things that matter most. To attempt this on our own invites the possibility not only of error but of arrogance. A wise minister will therefore discover or create two or three groups of people with whom the question of priorities can be kept under constant review. The freedom of being a minister in pastoral charge is burdensome, but burdens shared within the Christian family are also a privilege and a joy.

# Part I
# The Pastor Himself

# The Pastor and his Devotional Life

KENNETH LEECH, M.A.

Board for Social Responsibility, Church of England

A RECENT version of *Credo* (ITV, 9 March 1980) included a comment by a clergyman that, while, during the 1960s, churches were concerned with social and political change, this had now given way to an interest in prayer and spirituality, activities which, he said, could be carried on anywhere. While partially correct, it was a depressing and revealing comment, with its suggestion that not only were there two directions, the socio-political and the spiritual, distinct and perhaps even opposed, but also that prayer and spirituality somehow occur in a vacuum. The urgent issue today is not whether there is a resurgence of concern with spirituality, but whether this resurgence involves true spirituality or false. Elsewhere[1] I have suggested that much current spirituality, Christian and non-Christian, is in fact gnostic, and the spread of harmful and false spiritual tendencies has become very marked in recent years. The popularity of E. R. Norman's 1978 Reith Lectures, with their false polarization between 'true religion' which 'points to . . . the inward soul of man' and is concerned with the 'ethereal qualities of immortality', and false, 'politicized' religion concerned with 'social transformation', was typical of much fashionable reaction to the radicalizing trends of the 1960s.[2] Norman's position was widely mistaken for Christian orthodoxy. It is essential, therefore, in considering the spirituality of pastors, to identify criteria for discernment of true spirituality from false. I want to suggest that the spiritual life with which we are concerned cannot be a private segment of life, divorced from social and political concerns, but is rather the over-all direction of all life towards God and his kingdom. The purpose of ascetical discipline is to provide those external and internal resources, techniques and guidelines which will support such a direction. Spiritual life, devotional life, prayer life, is therefore a way of speaking about the pastor's whole life, orientated Godwards. So, writing of worship, Evelyn Underhill said:

> It stands for the total orientation of life towards God. . . . It is real in its own right, an action transcending and embracing all the separate souls taking part in it. The individual as such dies to his separate selfhood on entering the Divine society.[3]

But the life of prayer and worship must include consecrated times and spaces for concentrated prayer and reflection.

There are, however, a number of hindrances to the achievement of an integrated prayer life. One is a *functional* model of pastoral care. The pastor is seen as a functionary, a professional person who possesses skills and techniques which can be acquired by training, and he is concerned with using and allocating these skills and techniques in an efficient way. Efficiency, planning and the use of resources become central: in effect, the pastor becomes a manager, an administrator, a leader. This model has rightly been attacked by Holmes as one which excludes such roles as prayer and sacrament or assigns to them a low status.[4] They are only valued as a means to achieve some other end, ways to help us to do something else better. We need therefore to restore the centrality of prayer and adoration in the pastoral life. As Nouwen has said:

> Prayer is not a preparation for work or an indispensable condition for effective ministry. Prayer is life; prayer and ministry are the same and can never be divorced.[5]

A second hindrance is what Martin Thornton has called *multitudinism:* the loss of a sense of direction in pastoral work and its replacement by a vast range of unconnected and ever-increasing activities. In the midst of all this activity, the activity of prayer can easily be lost. And, of course, linked with this is a third hindrance, the fact of sheer *pressure of work* and demands, as well as intense emotional pressure which crushes the pastor into the ground, exhausts his spirit, undermines his prayer, and reduces the spiritual effectiveness of his ministry.

It is therefore essential that there should be, in every pastor's rule, a built-in dimension of contemplative stillness and reflection. The 'sabbath principle', the law of rest and re-creation, is vital, and its deliberate neglect is a grave sin whose results are all too apparent in broken lives and fragmented spirits. A life which is all activity and contains no contemplative element is seriously unbalanced: it is like a steel bridge with no give in it, and at some point it will snap. But contemplation is not simply a recipe for survival: it is itself the end, the purpose, of life. So St Augustine describes the City of God as a society in which God is adored for himself, in rest and in relaxation.

> All our activity will be Amen and Alleluia.
> There we shall rest and we shall see.
> We shall see and we shall love.
> We shall love and we shall praise.
> Behold what shall be in the end and shall not end. (*City of God*, Bk. 22.)

So I would insist on the necessity of a regular time of retreat (at least a week each year), a regular pattern of quiet days, and a pattern of 'mini-retreats' for study and prayer of several hours at a time. This last provision is most important. In very busy inner-city parishes in London in which I have worked (Hoxton 1964-7, Soho 1967-71,

Bethnal Green 1974-80) I have found that to carve out of each week a three-hour period of study, prayer and recollection, if necessary removing oneself physically to another place not too far away, is far more practical than just hoping that the odd half-hour at the beginning or end of the day will suffice and provide adequate spiritual nourishment.

The pressures on the inner-city pastor are considerable. He (or she) experiences the oppression of urbanism in a double way: first, in the way in which all the urban poor experience it, for few pastors are wealthy, however much they carry with them the privilege and power of the church machine; and, secondly, because he is constantly in demand and on call. Under such conditions pastors often become unhinged, their families break up, their resources dry up. When many others have saved and scrimped to get out, the urban pastor remains. But he may only remain as a spiritual skeleton, an exhausted, under-nourished shadow of a man. It is vital that the contemplative dimension of his ministry is not allowed to die. It is worth building up some kind of network by which each urban parish has its equivalent 'twin' in the countryside so that exchanges and rest periods can become a regular feature. Why cannot each inner-city pastor have his rural retreat by arrangement with a colleague there?

The curse of multitudinism is a threat to the life of prayer not only externally but also internally. There is too much noise and bustle in our heads. So there needs to be a reduction in the range of activity in the mind if a viable prayer rhythm is to be established. This involves the discipline of 'mind-fasting', avoiding mental overcrowding, and seeking a unification of mind and heart, what the Eastern Church calls 'taking the mind into the heart'. This simplifying of the mind is the purpose of the various types of meditation. Traditional techniques of meditation and 'spiritual exercises' are by no means out-dated and useless today. There has, for example, been a revival of the use of the Ignatian exercises in some places. But for many people today, disciplined reading leading to reflection and thence to prayer can be of more value than formal methods of meditation. The purpose of such disciplined reading, *lectio divina*, is to prepare the mind for prayer which is 'a laying aside of thought'. Books by contemporary authors, such as Thomas Merton, Aelred Squire or Simon Tugwell,[6] are useful in introducing and providing ways in which to learn from the 'great tradition'. From an evangelical standpoint, Richard Lovelace's recent study is very valuable.[7] But the chief importance of these books is that they send us back to the great teachers of the Christian tradition — to Gregory of Nyssa, Julian of Norwich, John of the Cross, John Wesley, and many others. It is essential that we realize, in our prayer, our solidarity with these guides and with the Body of Christ throughout the ages. In this connexion, the initiative of SPCK in introducing to the UK the Paulist Press library of spiritual classics is very much to be welcomed.

All spiritual guides stress the central place of silence. Whether on a daily or weekly basis, the practice of silence needs to be incorporated into our rule. The communities which have grown up around the Little Sisters and Brothers of Charles de Foucauld lay great emphasis on silent adoration. Again, the use of the Bible is a vital element in spiritual discipline. 'Bible study', while important, is not enough: there needs to be a prayerful 'brooding on the scriptures', in which we nourish our spirits on the divine word, or, in St Clement of Alexandria's words, 'feed from the breasts of the Logos'. Such disciplines as the recitation and learning of long passages of scripture are valuable in creating an interior dialogue between ourselves and the incarnate Word of God. One well-tried way of integrating adoration, silence, the use of scripture, and intercession is the use of some form of daily Office. The Divine Office is very ancient in Western and Eastern Christianity, and its revival in parts of post-Reformation Protestantism is a cause of rejoicing. The principal value of an Office is its objectivity: it is a way of sharing in the prayer of the whole Church, and is not dependent on our mood or subjective feelings, preferences and prejudices. The recitation of the Office by members of a family or a house community is a solid basis for daily prayer.

Yet it is the celebration of the Eucharist which is the heart of all Christian prayer and the source of Christian discipleship. The restoration of the sacrament to its rightful place as the centre of the week's worship and work is important both for the building up of the Christian community and for the nourishment of each individual. The Eucharist is the heart of 'Christian materialism': it 'earths' our spirituality, anchors us in the common life, and provides our personal striving with its social context.

Finally, there are a number of practical aspects of the devotional life which need brief mention.

(i) The value of *fasting* as an element of prayer and a stimulus to action.

(ii) The importance of learning from the writings of Christians of previous centuries and other continents, and allowing them to broaden our vision.

(iii) The value of having a *'soul friend'*, a spiritual guide, to whom we can bear our sorrows and share our joys.[8]

(iv) The value of a *prayer notebook,* a personal collection of thoughts and prayers; or, if one uses a loose-leaf diary, of including one's prayers and intercessions within it so that prayer and daily activity are mingled. (The Filofax diary system, obtainable from Norman and Hill, Plough Yard, Bishopsgate, London EC2 is very easy to use in this way, and has become popular among the clergy in East London.)

(v) The value of some link with a *religious community* or place of retreat to which one can go regularly for refreshment and renewal, and which one can see as a spiritual home.

(vi) The willingness to learn from other Christian traditions and from non-Christians about ways of building up interior prayer and continuous recollection of the presence of God.

---

[1] Leech, Kenneth, *Youthquake: spirituality and the Counter-Culture* (Sheldon Press [1973]).

[2] Norman, E. R., *Christianity and the World Order* (OUP [1979]).

[3] Underhill, Evelyn, *Worship* (Nisbet [1936]), 84, 86.

[4] Holmes, Urban T., *The Future Shape of Ministry* (Seabury Press, N.Y. [1971]).

[5] Nouwen, Henri J. M., *Creative Ministry* (Image Books, N.Y. [1978]).

[6] Merton, Thomas, *Contemplative Prayer* (Darton, Longman & Todd [1973]). Squire, Aelred, *Asking the Fathers* (SPCK [1976]). Tugwell, Simon, *Prayer*. 2 vols. (Veritas, Dublin [1974]). Cf. Leech, Kenneth, *True Prayer: an Introduction to Christian Spirituality* (Sheldon Press [1980]).

[7] Lovelace, Richard, *Dynamics of Spiritual Life* (Paternoster Press [1979]).

[8] Leech, Kenneth, *Soul Friend: a study in Spirituality* (Sheldon Press [1977]).

# Maintaining Reading and Study

BRUCE GRAINGER, B.A.
Baildon, Yorkshire

## Identifying the Problem

MOST clergy and ministers pay lip service at least to academic work by having a room somewhere which they call a study. According to the OED this is 'a room used for literary occupation, transaction of business, etc.' At Theological College I was advised to spend an hour or two each day in there reading, and Archdeacon Forder writes that 'even pastoral work should not steal the time allocated to study'.[1] I am writing this in my study, well-lined with books, but not all read very much. I am also surrounded by office equipment, typewriters, duplicator, photocopier and so on, and much of the table space is currently taken up with copies of the Lesson Readers and Offertory Procession rota, the sidesmen's rota and a special service for tomorrow evening for the local Council of Churches. The transaction of business is often in danger of cramping out the literary occupation because, like many other minister's studies, this is also a parish office, and it is a sad fact that clergy and ministers working in full time pastoral jobs can probably do much of what is expected of them without much systematic reading and study. People are more likely to notice our transaction of business than our study of recent theology. It is very easy to get out of the way of regular reading and study when we have a roof and six ancient gargoyles to support, job rotas to produce, the elderly and ill to visit, and large numbers of baptisms, weddings and funerals to arrange and follow up.

Although children in our local school felt sure their Vicar spent a lot of time at home writing sermons, much sermon preparation can be undertaken without a lot of academic effort, and does not necessarily occupy hours of time. Many of us are not lost for words in the pulpit and it can be argued that ordinary people wouldn't appreciate anything which seemed too theological anyway.

All this adds up to a powerful disincentive to reading and study. If ministers are to maintain regular reading and study, or perhaps more likely, take it up again, strong incentives are needed. Dr Samuel Johnson remarked that 'when a man knows he is to be hanged in a fortnight, it concentrates his mind wonderfully'. Some of us have minds wonderfully concentrated on study when we realize that we have to give a series of lectures in a fortnight and prepare an advance synopsis for students. Although this is a strong incentive it doesn't usually lead me into systematic study. Rather it emphasizes the problem of having so many different involvements both inside and outside our parishes or areas of pastoral responsibility.

## Towards a Theology of Study

Recently Anglican clergy from the Diocese of Bradford held a conference at which one of the speakers was David Jenkins, then Professor at the University of Leeds, and I am grateful to him for helping me to clarify my ideas on the role of the pastoral minister and the role of the professional theologian. We looked at the sharing of ministry. We considered how the minister is set apart but how also he cannot be seen as an authoritative single figure.

Some clergy undoubtedly think in terms of a sacerdotal role in a society which they assume is at least tinged with Christianity. Whether they are called priests or ministers of religion, they are set apart to speak for man to God and for God to man. This can lead to a very isolated role, especially in areas where clergy are thin on the ground, and the isolated priest is likely to see his study and reading in isolation — something which he does (or perhaps does not do) but for himself and for his own ministry.

Some clergy prefer to think of themselves as 'parsons'. This could mean that they are simply trying to be themselves — open to others and relating to others, and if so they will also see themselves as accountable to others and learning from others. They will still have a distinctive role — in fact the Latin word *persona* comes to mean a role — but reading and study in this context will not simply be to raise the minister's own horizons. They are to read and study because they have a responsibility to the whole Body of Christ as well as to their fellow ministers to understand as deeply as possible the things of God. This includes trying to understand current thought in theology and to ask what the Holy Spirit is saying in any situation. The minister is not therefore to give up regular reading and study on the grounds that his own particular pastoral responsibility does not seem to warrant it.

The professional theologian fits into this shared ministry as someone who has special responsibility for the church's tradition and all its ramifications and complexities. He will look for the things God wants us to work out in our generation and to which God expects a response. He will present his findings for others to study. Seen in this light, someone who does not bother to read or to study systematically is going to limit the application of what God is saying today. In an important sense, the parish priest or minister is in the front line when it comes to working out theological insights, and he will have a role as an enabler of lay people who have not had the same opportunities for reading and study because of their full-time secular occupations. If he does not himself read widely, he is likely to indoctrinate lay people with some narrow party line, so giving them a view of Christianity which makes it out to be an ideology.

So far I have made it seem as if all reading and study should be to do with theology. In practice this can't possibly be so. In order to apply any theological insights in a pastoral situation, the pastor must keep in touch with what is going on in the world at large and must make an effort to understand the real concerns of those to whom he is ministering and how experts in other fields identify and analyse these concerns. In a lecture entitled 'Renewing of my Faith' Canon Sydney Evans expressed it in this way: 'Are you or are you not glad to be a man living in the world of today? To read Peter Brown's brilliant study of St Augustine and to read Desmond Morris' *The Naked Ape* side by side is an illuminating thing to do. To do this is to pose in the sharpest way the question — "what then does it mean to live in our world today by the insights and commitment of Christian Faith?".'[2]

## Providing good Incentives

Archdeacon Forder quotes Dewar and Hudson, *A Manual of Pastoral Psychology*, in which the authors lay equal stress on the need for mental and physical efficiency and show that a disciplined mind, a good memory, and power of concentration are within the range of any parish priest. The way to achieve this happy state of efficiency doesn't involve answering an advertisement in a Sunday newspaper and sending for a crash course in retentive reading, but, they believe, in simply getting on with reading and study. 'Changing of occupation to study is a real rest and does not lead to fatigue.' So much then, seems to depend on personal discipline. Dewar and Hudson also say that 'if any clergyman is tempted to think that he cannot concentrate because of unfavourable conditions, let him see to it that he becomes independent of them as quickly as possible'.[3] Many of us nowadays find it almost impossible to become independent of constant interruptions from the telephone and from personal callers.

I believe that the church as a whole should recognize that clergy simply cannot be expected nowadays to have to go it alone when it comes to maintaining reading and study, and that in any case this is not the right attitude. Some pastors may be able to study in spite of today's distractions but the church has to recognize that what is needed is a corporate system of continuing training for clergy, and that this is essential for the renewal of the church. It should also be possible for lay people to participate, and the whole system should be regarded as adult religious education. In fact this is what is now beginning to happen in many places. Many Anglican dioceses, for example, have an Adult Education Adviser who arranges courses and groups. Junior clergy are likely to have three years of compulsory post-ordination training consisting of group discussion based on reading, investigation of practical problems encountered in ministry, and some personal tuition geared to the needs of the individual clergyman. It may soon come to be regarded as the norm for all ministers to be involved with adult education, perhaps even by direction from the church hierarchy. As a school governor, and also as a former teacher myself, I am impressed with the sort of courses that serving teachers attend to give them deeper insights into their subjects and to help them to understand new developments in education. Application forms to be filled in by teachers seeking new appointments usually ask for details of courses attended and qualifications and skills gained since leaving college or university, and a form I have on my desk at present asks for this information to be given under the headings, Full time, Part time, and In-Service.

All three kinds of courses can be arranged for clergy to keep them up to date with theology and to enable them to re-think their faith. These courses provide the right sort of stimulus for continued reading and study.

I believe that we should look forward to the time when what is considered to be right for teachers, is applied to ministers who would be expected to provide evidence of courses attended. To make this possible for all those in the pastoral ministry the churches would have to see it as a corporate responsibility, so that replacements can be arranged for any clergyman on sabbatical leave. In the Anglican Church it would be wrong if only clergy in parishes with curates could take any sort of study leave. There is, I am sure, a danger in thinking that renewal in the church can be brought about simply by sending its ministers on courses, but the danger of being out of touch and insular with no incentives to regular reading and study is far, far worse.

Is it far fetched to expect that clergy might be able to give details such as these when they are being considered for new appointments?

Courses attended and any other qualifications obtained since leaving College:

Full time:    Five weeks sabbatical leave at X Theological College 1980 studying Role of the Church in an Industrial Society.

Part time:   Wholeness and man's relationship to his world — September — November 1978.

In-Service:  Bradford Seminar on Religious Studies — Spring 1979. Working with groups — four weekly sessions — May 1980.

There is plenty of scope for such courses to be interdenominational and this in any case, makes it easier to obtain well-qualified leaders for the courses.

It is quite feasible for clergy and ministers to arrange far more self-help than at present. As it becomes more and more the norm for them to become part of study courses, so it might lead to increasing numbers of informal study groups to stimulate continued study and reading and a wider sharing of important insights. This type of self-help can produce a balance between subjects which an adult education officer or a visiting theologian thinks ought to be studied, and subjects which local clergy feel are directly related to the work they do in their parishes. Such groups could also provide useful feedback for experts who may know relatively little about the parochial ministry.

I am sure that lay people should be involved as far as possible alongside clergy both in organizing courses and groups and also as members of them. The Canterbury Consultation of 1969 had this to say: 'There was general concern for far more adult religious education. One report said that while plain information about the faith is required, particularly in respect of information about the church, clergy and laity must learn from each other. Training by the group method for laity and clergy was suggested in a report which said that in-service training of the clergy, also by the group method, should even be by direction from the bishop.'[4]

All these considerations emphasize the corporate responsibility of clergy and laity for study to renew and to build up the Body of Christ.

### Knowing what to read

Thomas Carlyle wrote that 'what printed thing soever I could meet with I read'.[5] Had he been alive today, he might have been overwhelmed with the huge numbers of books being published each year, including, it seems, more religious titles than ever before. There is no shortage of material but it has become more and more difficult to decide what to read as most of us have less time available for reading than clergy had in the nineteenth century. As students we were no doubt given book lists related to the subjects to be studied and if we underwent any form of post-ordination training we would probably have continued to have our reading directed for several more years. After this it is generally assumed that we will have developed the reading habit and will be able to decide for ourselves what to read in future. For religious books, the various church newspapers and periodicals provide regular and helpful book reviews which often have the advantage of being written by ministers who are doing similar work to our own, although I am a little discouraged when I think how many books David Edwards must read for his *Church Times* reviews, and how few I get through. The *Expository Times* contains short reviews of over five hundred books each year. Publishing houses send regular book catalogues to all who are on their mailing lists and these are often divided into general subjects such as Biblical Interpretation, Social Responsibility, Mission and Unity, Prayer and Devotion, Education, and so on. The catalogues contain brief summaries of the contents and occasional excerpts from favourable reviews.

However, as has been proposed earlier, reading and study should be a corporate responsibility accepted by the church as an important ingredient leading towards renewal. If clergy can be encouraged more and more to take part in courses and do-it-yourself study groups then more of their reading will be related to this. Study courses by themselves will not bring about renewal in the church, neither are they the answer to our individual problems with reading and study, but they provide incentives. They can also give coherence to study and guard against haphazard buying of books which remain largely unread because they were not well chosen. Junior Anglican clergy, and probably those of other denominations are often supervised by a tutor for some three years after ordination. One of the tutor's responsibilities is to advise on books to read related to individual need and interest. Many more senior clergy would probably welcome friendly advice on what to read and in their turn would be prepared to discuss choice of books with others. Many churches nowadays run a church bookstall which, in the hands of an efficient manager, promotes reading and study in the congregation. Judging from a number of church magazines and newsletters, the minister may be expected to write reviews to encourage lay people to read religious books. An Anglican Archdeacon recently encouraged his clergy to read by sending them all a complimentary copy of a book which he felt they ought to study, bought in quantity at a large discount. At the same time he helped a local bookshop to get rid of a title which had not until then reached the forecast sales level.

An obvious problem is the cost of books. Ministers do not always make full use of library facilities which are available. Local libraries are often prepared to buy requested titles, colleges of education as well as universities allow use of their library and resource facilities.

## Profitable Servants

The image of the ordained minister is interlinked with the image of Jesus Christ who took the form of a servant, and the pastoral ministry involves caring for others at ground level. The form of a servant may mean, as Canon Eric James has written, in part the form of a civil servant,[6] but a major part is also to have effective dialogue with people who, though perhaps estranged from the church, are nevertheless becoming more and more articulate. If the minister is to speak effectively, he must understand what is going on in the church and especially what God may be saying to the church today. He is also called to help train better qualified lay people, and to be an enabler and a reconciler. To fill this role effectively he must wait on God and use his intellect through effective reading and study.

[1] C. R. Forder: *The Parish Priest at Work* (SPCK), 33.

[2] *Faith, Ministry, Unity,* report of Canterbury Consultation 1969, 37.

[3] Dewar & Hudson: *A Manual of Pastoral Psychology,* 76, quoted by C. R. Forder, 33.

[4] Canterbury Consultation, 59.

[5] Thomas Carlyle: *Sartor Resartus,* bk. ii, ch. 3.

[6] E. James: *Odd Man Out* (Hodder & Stoughton), 85.

# The Pastor and his Bible

HENRY McKEATING, M.Th., Ph.D.
University of Nottingham

THERE are three obvious areas in which the minister is involved with the Bible. First, there is his own thinking and devotion. Second, there is preaching and worship. Third, there is teaching, which may take place in fellowship groups or lay training sessions. Teaching may also go on in sermons and services of worship. Teaching and proclamation are logically distinct but in practice are often closely associated, as the NT itself illustrates. These areas are all interrelated, but for the sake of order it will be best to look at them separately.

Area number one is vital: the pastor can only teach what he knows, only preach what he has grasped or been grasped by. When he expounds scripture in the pulpit he can only *say* what the scripture has *said to him*. He cannot expect the Bible to be central to the life and thinking of his people if it is not central to his own.

As ministers we have received expensive theological educations, involving very substantial amounts of biblical study. Too many of us have made too little of what we have been offered. The biblical study which we did in our initial training was not the enrichment that it should have been. During that training we are fed with biblical knowledge over a period of two or three years, or even more, and then too often get up into our pulpits and preach as if we knew none of it. We have 'learnt' it well enough to pass our examinations, but too many of us have not really allowed it to affect our own *thinking* about the Bible. We have not made the knowledge our own.

The reasons why all this happens are complex, and cannot be fully dealt with in this short article, but two things may briefly be said. First, some of us fail to get the best out of our biblical study because we perceive critical study as a threat, as destructive. But critical study of the Bible has only one concern, with truth. And the kind of faith that feels threatened by truth is not a very desirable kind anyway. Truth can never take us further from God, for God is truth. And if truth turns out to be more complicated than we thought, and to be destructive of our comforting simplicities, we do God no honour by remaining with the simplicities. To learn more of truth must in the end be a liberating and an enriching experience, though in the short run it may well be a frightening one.

The second observation is in fact closely tied up with the first. Some of us have not assimilated the results of our critical study as thoroughly as we might because at the bottom of our minds we still think of it as an optional extra. There is a common assumption that biblical study can be done on two levels: there is first of all a 'simple' understanding of the content of the Bible itself, and then a second stage of academic or critical understanding for those clever enough to cope with such things. One hears ministers or ordinands speak of their 'devotional use' of the Bible and their 'Bible study' as if these were not only separate but unrelated activities. Anyone who makes this sharp distinction is failing to let either half of his Bible reading activity profit from the other half, and both must be impoverished. When we 'study' the Bible, even if it is the problems of Greek grammar that are uppermost in our minds at the time, it is still the Word of God which we are studying and God can still speak to us through it. A gospel writer's subtle choice of a particular verbal tense may be highly significant for what God wishes to say *now*. If we want to know what the Bible is saying to us in the twentieth century our understanding of it must be a critical understanding *from the start*. Critical understanding cannot be applied as 'topping' to the existing cake of our biblical knowledge. We must understand the Bible critically and historically, in the context of its own times, that we may with more certainty see what it is saying to ours.

The historical study of the Bible is sometimes criticized as if it were simply a sort of antiquarianism, but it is surely a necessary precursor, though no more than a precursor, to our asking the question about what the Bible means to us now. What Isaiah's words meant *to Isaiah* and to Isaiah's contemporaries, which is the historical question, can surely never be irrelevant to us, even though it will frequently not be sufficient for us. Isaiah's words may mean more to us than they meant to Isaiah; they can surely never mean less.

The Word of God is both thoroughly human and thoroughly divine. Not to make the effort to find out what it meant in its original historical context is to fail to take seriously its human dimension. Conversely, of course, to find out what it meant in its original historical context and then to assume that that is all that needs to be done is to forget altogether that it is the word of God with which we are dealing.

A great deal of patient, historical study has to be pursued if much of the Bible these days is to speak to us at all. The reason is the self-evident one of the tremendous pace of change. It is commonly said, and truly, that life has changed more in the last two hundred years than in the previous two thousand. The consequences of this for our understanding of the Bible are enormous. Language which spoke directly and compellingly to people of biblical times still for the most part spoke as directly and as comprehensibly to the people of the middle ages, or of the reformation period, or to those of Wesley's England. Much of the same language speaks a great deal less directly now. Biblical images, which were chosen because they spoke with an immediacy which explained all, are become now things that themselves need explanation. Because of the gap between our world and that of the Bible, a gap whose increase in size accelerates with every year that passes, it becomes harder and harder simply to pick up a Bible and make sense of it.

The pastor has the training, and must make the time, to bridge this gap. He must bridge it *for himself;* find out for himself what God is saying *to him* through the scriptures, and thus 'deliver his own soul'. And then he has an extra job, to mediate that knowledge to his people in preaching and teaching. More and more the pastor is needed as a mediator. God speaks through the scriptures, but much of the language in which he speaks is in urgent need of an interpreter. Do not let us exaggerate: happily, there are still passages of scripture which speak for themselves better than any of their interpreters will ever speak for them. But more and more of our people need help even to find where such passages are.

This mediatorial role which is thrust upon us is peculiarly regrettable to those of us brought up in the Protestant tradition, for which the accessibility and sufficiency of holy scripture have always been of fundamental importance. It has always been our conviction that, provided that he could read his own language, 'the boy that followeth the plough' could understand enough of scripture to lead him to salvation. But few of us any longer follow ploughs, and what was sufficiently intelligible to 'the boy that followeth the plough' is less and less intelligible to the man that mindeth the machine or the operative that programmeth the computer. And this, no doubt, is a reason why some of us are attracted to older and simpler attitudes to the Bible, and have a craving for ancient certainties, because the position we find ourselves in, standing *between* the people and the Bible, is one that is *theologically* offensive to us. We find ourselves obliged to do a job which Protestants have traditionally asserted did not need to be done. But, theologically offensive or not, the job does need to be done. The pastor finds himself occupying a position which he has never needed to occupy since the advent of universal literacy. His training and his knowledge are the lens, through which his people are enabled to read the print that it increasingly strains their minds to read unaided. The traditional role of the Protestant pastor and preacher is to point people to the Word, and invite them to read for themselves the saving truth. But more and more turn back to him echoing the Ethiopian's reply to Philip: 'How can I [understand] unless someone guides me?' (Acts 8[31]).

Most of the pastor's people will be aware of the Bible primarily in the context of worship. In that context it will be read and it will be expounded. The reading of the lessons is not merely a ritual precursor to the preaching of the sermon. Gone are the days when a preacher could assume that in reading the lessons he was running through words which were already likely to be thoroughly familiar to the majority of his listeners. The preparation of the lessons is more important than it ever was.

Choice of the best translation for the immediate purpose is important. We all have our favourite translations, but it is worth cross-checking to see if a different one is better for our particular reading. Some local churches are trying to standardize by recommending a particular version for regular use. Where such arrangements exist they should be honoured if at all possible. They are often part of a scheme to encourage Bible reading by providing Bibles in the pews, and it helps if the congregation can follow in the same version as the preacher reads. It is a sign of the times that where Bibles are provided in the pews many worshippers are grateful for a page reference as well as chapter and verse.

But above all, most lessons benefit from a couple of sentences (it need rarely be more) of introduction. Even the tiniest bit of background, or the smallest hint of what to look for in the passage, makes a great deal of difference, not just to whether the people understand, but to whether they listen or not.

To come to the sermon: it is the preacher's job, no less than that of his people, to 'sit under the Word', i.e., to respect the Word and to listen to what it has to say. The text is not to be used as an excuse for trotting out what *we* want to say.

It might be useful at this point to mention the much-debated use of lectionaries. I have gone on record elsewhere as expressing doubts about the rationale behind lectionaries. Certainly it would be desirable to have something much more rationally structured and more comprehensive than the JLG lectionary which most of our churches have officially adopted. But until we get such an improved scheme there is something to be said, not for slavishly following a lectionary month in month out when God is offering us more urgent things to preach about, but for the discipline that a lectionary can provide. A lectionary makes the preacher consider texts which it would not otherwise have occurred to him to preach about. It brings together lessons which he would not unaided have associated. It forces on his attention passages which, unprompted, he might never have turned to. All of these make it more likely that he will actually listen to the Word rather than impose his ideas and preferences *on* the Word. It is worth remarking that if there are tracts of scripture which a Christian finds especially unexciting and unrewarding, let him pay them particular attention. It may be that the Lord is saying to him in those uncongenial portions something which he does not want to hear.

But listening to what the Word is saying is not the same as merely repeating what we find in scripture. The pastor with a proof text for all occasions may reassure some, but he will be felt profoundly unhelpful by many. Part of the problem of interpreting the Bible in the twentieth century is that we face innumerable situations and problems which in biblical times had never even been imagined, and which the Bible therefore never directly or explicitly deals with. To answer these by reaching for the nearest text which looks on the surface as if it might serve may lead to dangerous simplifications and indeed falsifications of the biblical message.

A clear example of this is the way some Christians settle a whole range of problematical questions, about abortion, about capital punishment, about war, simply by quoting 'Thou shalt not kill', regardless of the fact that the biblical writers themselves make it very evident that they do not see the commandment as inconsistent with either judicial execution or killing in war. Few of us, no doubt, are quite so simple minded, but we do the same thing more subtly and in relation to other issues.

Interpretation is a much more complex business than the finding of proof texts. For one thing, a proper listening to the Word involves looking for the thrust of the biblical tradition *as a whole*. But more important, it involves a *dialogue* between the Bible and its interpreter in which the interpreter has something to bring *to* the Bible as well as something to learn from it. For the Bible is part of the same living tradition in which we ourselves stand. It is not merely the datum which we interpret, but is itself the product of interpretation. It is a series of layers of tradition, each

interpreting those that went before. The Chronicler reinterprets the traditions of Samuel and Kings, the Priestly writer
reinterprets those of the Yahwist, Isaiah's disciples offer
reinterpretations for new times of the traditions of their
master. The NT reinterprets and re-evaluates all the
traditions of the OT together. St John reinterprets
traditions which already existed in the synoptics. One could
give examples endlessly. This is the clear picture which
emerges from critical study of the Bible, and it has a
powerful moral for what we are doing when we expound the
scriptures. It means that when we ascend the pulpit steps to
expound Isaiah or St Paul we are doing something which is
not different in kind from what the prophet or the apostle
himself did. The words he offered were an interpretation
and an application to his own time of the tradition he had
received. His words are themselves now part of the tradition
*we* have received, and we too interpret and apply.

This does not make us *equal* with the authors of
scripture, but it does make us fellow-workers in the same
task. And it means too that no one can preach scripture as
the Word of God unless he stands within the community
which produced scripture and for whom it was produced,
and unless he shares in some measure the inspiration of the
same Spirit. Inspired scripture, if it is to speak to the heart
of any generation, requires inspired interpreters.

A corollary of this is that we cannot merely pick up the
words of scripture and reissue them unchanged. It is not
enough to lift Amos's message to eighth-century Israel and
redeliver it to twentieth-century Britain. As Amos delivered
it, it was God's Word to that society at that time. Merely to
repeat Amos's words does not make them God's Word to
our society in our time. The interpreter has much more to
do than that. It is tempting to read Amos's words and then
ask, 'Are Amos's judgments on his society appropriate to

our society?' Possibly some of them are, but it is the wrong question with which to begin. We need to ask: *'How did Amos know* what was the Word of God to his society? How did he arrive at his judgments?' Then we must see if we can learn from him how *we* might discover the Word of God to *our* generation.

To put all this another way: when we approach the Bible with our twentieth-century questions, over and over again we find that it does not offer us answers. What we do find, if we are patient, is that it offers us clues as to how the answers might be arrived at; i.e., it does not offer us answers, but methods by which answers may be found.

This is perhaps one of the points at which our Protestant principles have been a snare to us. We have been so concerned to exalt the dignity and authority of scripture that we have forgotten the authority of the community of faith, which alone can tell us what scripture means. We shall get better interpretation from our pulpits when we have restored the dignity of the interpreter.

Finally, let us look at Bible *teaching.* The need for such teaching will have emerged from much that has already been said. The cheering thing for the teacher of the Bible is what a long way a little knowledge sometimes goes. People can be enormously helped in their understanding of the Bible by being given some very elementary pieces of information. Historical information, for example, may be very valuable. The stories in the book of Daniel make much, much better sense as soon as they are seen against the background of the Maccabaean persecutions. Some elementary information about the way books of the Bible took shape can be equally useful. It can be very illuminating just to point out that a prophetic book is rarely put together in chronological order, but that the compilers tended to group oracles by subject matter; oracles of condemnation, oracles of hope, oracles against foreign nations, and so on. If such information only helps by removing false expectations it achieves something.

One does not need to go into the technicalities of biblical criticism, but it *is* necessary from the start to use a critical approach. In preaching, the pastor should certainly not preach biblical criticism; but he should certainly not preach as though biblical criticism did not exist. In teaching, some presentation of critical knowledge itself is appropriate and useful. The synoptic problem stares any reader of the Bible in the face. To spell out, in outline, the nature of the problem and the sort of relationship that is believed to exist between the gospels is well worth doing, and it must make for more informed listening and reading.

In preaching and worship we tend to offer the Bible in short passages, and preach from individual verses. In teaching one can look at a broader canvas. The structure of a whole book can carry a message that none of its individual parts carries. And there is a need to sketch out, from time to time, the whole story of salvation as the Bible presents it. Most of us do far too little of this kind of teaching, and our people find it very revealing when we do.

The scholar (and the scholar, of course, is usually just the pastor wearing a different hat) will pursue his historical and critical knowledge for its own sake. And he *must* do so, if he is to be sure of finding out the truth. Some of his people may well find such knowledge fascinating for its own sake too, but with most of them he will be wise to be selective. In his own reading and study he cannot afford to be selective. For the pastor to attempt to confine his reading to what will be most directly useful for preaching is futile, because he doesn't know what will be useful until he has digested it. To attempt to follow any such policy will simply ensure that in any existing areas of ignorance he will remain ignorant.

Again he must not shirk his part as filter, or mediator. He will be selective in what he passes on, for he will only pass on what positively helps in making sense of scripture, and he will pass on first what helps most. Of each piece of knowledge he should ask: 'How much "mileage" will my congregation get from this?' As I hope I have illustrated, some quite small pieces of knowledge have a great deal of 'mileage' in them. He should try to think back to his own days of relative ignorance of biblical matters and ask himself: 'What knowledge did I myself find most helpful in making sense of the Bible?'

I have spoken up to now as if the pastor was always the authority figure, always the one who knows, the one with the skill and expertise. Every pastor knows that this is not so. In terms of technical knowledge the pastor is likely to be better equipped than most of his folk (though his congregation may well contain some people more expert than he). In terms of insight and spiritual awareness this is unlikely to be so. It is more than probable that some members of his church will have a longer, a deeper and more mature Christian experience than his own. Not only will he learn from them, if he is willing to listen, but he will be able to learn too from those less mature in Christian things than himself. To understand the Word of God is in the last resort a communal activity. The pastor should be able to *lead* his people in this endeavour, but in the end they must grow in understanding *together* if they are to grow at all.

# Part II
# The Pastor in Church

# The Pastor at Worship

J. DAVID BRIDGE, B.A., B.D.

London

WERE I a minister with responsibility for leading worship in the same local church week by week I know what my initial reaction would be on picking up an article on worship by someone whose present circumstances make it unlikely that he will ever confront the same congregation more than once in five years. It was therefore with more than usual reluctance that I accepted the editor's invitation to develop a paragraph from an earlier article entitled 'A Pastor's Priorities'. There I wrote that a pastor's role must be 'to initiate and play a creative part' in worship, and I suggested that this does not always mean taking the lead in acts of worship. Now I am challenged to say more precisely what that means. I respond, despite the misgivings already referred to, because my experience on the staff of the Methodist Home Mission Division and therefore a peripatetic preacher has reinforced my earlier convictions as a circuit minister that worship has been allowed to become too much the exclusive concern of professionals and needs now to be restored to the people of God.

My thesis is a simple one, that we all have a gift or gifts which can enable us and others to worship. The time has come for these gifts to be released and deployed. This can only happen when those entrusted by tradition or church law with responsibility for worship take initiatives which surrender their exclusive status. In worship as in so much else, the pastor must be an enabler and a liberator.

My thesis is also an urgent one. It should be apparent to

anyone whose experience of worship is not confined to traditional services in mainstream churches that there has grown up an 'alternative culture' in Christian worship. Shaped by such diverse influences as the charismatic movement, theories of group dynamics, and what we might call the 'spirit of the 1960s' this alternative worship manifests itself regularly through the house group movement and occasionally at a major festival, gathering, or assembly. Through worship of this kind many people have become Christians and many more have found their faith come to life, discovering excitement and inspiration where previously there was just routine. This can only be a cause for joy; but a cause for concern is that this alternative worship finds little or no echo in the regular life of our established churches. This must lead, unless a process of convergence takes place, to the serious impoverishment of the church.

In the Free Church tradition the minister or appointed lay preacher has absolute authority over the conduct of worship, subject only to restrictions imposed by trust deed and church law. In the last resort this is a wise and necessary arrangement; the problem is that it too easily becomes a matter of the first resort. Ministers have shown the greatest reluctance to involve their people even in thinking about worship let alone conducting it. Worship has become like all-in wrestling, a matter for professionals and spectators. Only a providential succession of tone-deaf clergy has allowed congregations to continue to sing hymns and there are churches where even this function has been taken from the people and handed over to a trained choir.

If you think the case is being over-stated you might consider how often as a visiting preacher you are able to have a real conversation about worship with stewards in the vestry before a service begins. I find it to be a rare experience, the response to any question being invariably, 'We leave that to you'. When I persist and enquire, 'What is your thinking about . . . the place of the offertory or the presence of children?' it is evident that there has been little beyond a concern that the latter shall not drop the former.

This is not an essay about worship, it is a consideration of how worship may be restored to the people. This will involve on the part of ministers a willingness to let go something of their traditional authority, and on the part of lay people a willingness to assume responsibility. The two processes will normally go hand in hand, but the initiative is with the minister as one who is called both to enable people to worship and to release their gifts.

My personal liberation came through the development of family worship. Our practice, which developed over a number of years, was to choose the theme of the service three months in advance. We then farmed it out to all the young people's groups within the church, Sunday School, youth club, uniformed organizations, etc., with the request that they might begin to think about an aspect of the theme and discover ways of expressing it in worship. With a month to go we met together and pooled our ideas. The shape of a service began to emerge and my role in the remaining weeks was simply to enable these ideas to come together in coherent and feasible form for sharing with the whole church. The result was the offering of liturgical material that I could never in my wildest dreams have imagined. I could not have scripted the role play devised by ten-year olds, nor could I have performed the conjuring tricks required by the cub scouts to celebrate a God who works surprisingly, or the dances created by the guides to express compassion or joy or hope. Before long questions were being asked about the essential definition of worship, and the only answer which made sense to us was whatever expresses our relationship with a transcendent God.

It should not be thought that only special gifts have a place in worship. There is a contribution to be made by the specially gifted, and we shall discuss this in a moment, but the most important offering is ourselves. The supreme task of the creator of worship is to enable people to offer themselves. In part this means offering their thought. Every church should have some regular opportunity for its members to talk together about worship and so both understand and influence its nature and shape. Sometimes worship has a shape but it is hidden from people; hymns are announced, lessons are read, prayers are offered, but how they relate to each other and to the sermon is a mystery known only to the preacher and to God. How much more helpful it is to arrange the printed order of service in sections whose headings indicate the pattern; e.g., A time of adoration — God's   challenge — Our   response — Our concern for others. In addition to thinking about the shape and content of their worship, congregations could share in many other ways than by singing and listening. Many people feel much happier about speaking rather than singing but rarely have an opportunity to do so through a responsive reading or a psalm. It is sometimes thought that Free Church congregations have an aversion to responsive readings. The truth is probably that they soon tire of the same responsive readings week after week, but this should not discourage us from seeking out or even creating responsive readings which fit particular circumstances.

Congregations also contribute a great deal by the preparation they bring to worship. Do we help them as much as we might? One church known to me bases its morning worship on the lectionary and prints each Sunday's appointed lessons on the previous week's announcement sheet. Many of the congregation come to worship having already immersed themselves in the biblical passages for the day. That leads me to the question of the use of the Bible by the congregation. It is generally thought that the sight of worshippers following the scripture passage in their own copies of the Bible indicates a high degree of spirituality and seriousness. My attitude to this is somewhat ambiguous; when in the pulpit I am encouraged by the sight of people using their own Bibles, but when in the congregation I never do this, finding it a distraction. In fact I find I can concentrate best on the Bible reading if my eyes are closed but am hesitant to do this for fear of being misunderstood. What is not in doubt is that preachers should encourage those who wish to use their own Bibles to do so, by announcing the reading in such a way that worshippers have ample time to find the right place.

Few churches encourage their congregations to do more in prayer than to sit quietly. The very least we should do is to enable people to offer requests for prayer, either through a suggestion box in the vestibule or in some other way. Requests can then be shared by written or printed announcement. The question of open prayer by congregations is more vexed and very often it is architecture rather than tradition which militates against it. However, where there are flexible seating arrangements and where the ethos of the congregation would support it, time spent in small groups in which people are able to pray openly as they feel led, can be an effective and enriching experience.

With some imagination, many more ways can be perceived in which people with no special gifts can share more positively in worship. Take the service of agape or love-feast for example. At the heart of this service is the belief that sharing food together can be an act of worship. So the congregation are asked to bring a picnic to worship. Because some will come unprepared people are asked to bring enough for two. At an appropriate point in the service people share and eat, remembering some of the many occasions in the NT when the offering of food revealed the presence of God.

Another example of a service whose main resource is people and a sanctified imagination comes from Notting Hill. On Palm Sunday in the Methodist Church there, palm crosses are distributed to the congregation who are invited to take and keep them as a sign of discipleship and their willingness to follow Jesus. The following year on Ash Wednesday the congregation gather again to confess their failures in discipleship. They bring with them their crosses from the previous year and as they enter the sanctuary these crosses are placed in a large dustbin as a sign of penitence. During the first part of the service the crosses are burnt as a symbol of the blotting out of past sin. Some crosses have previously been burned and their ashes are in a bowl on the communion table. The ministers kneel at the communion rail and a member of the congregation makes with the ashes the sign of the cross on their foreheads, saying, 'Lord have mercy'. The ministers respond, 'Christ have mercy'. Members of the congregation are then invited to come forward to receive the mark of the cross in the same way. Later in the service, after the prayer of thanksgiving and before the bread and wine are received in Holy Communion, the congregation exchange the Peace. As each one greets his or her neighbour, 'The peace of the Lord', the mark of the cross is wiped away as a sign of forgiveness and reconciliation.

We turn to examine some of the more specialized gifts which may in appropriate circumstances help others to worship. The words 'appropriate circumstances' are important because a casual reading of the list that follows might give the impression that what is being advocated is a restoration of the Chelsea Arts Ball. Every gift offered in worship must be offered with sensitivity, both towards God and towards other worshippers. Anything offered purely as a novelty becomes a gimmick and is unworthy of worship. Anything which alienates other worshippers threatens fellowship and achieves the opposite of what is intended. What follows are elements of worship which are generally neglected and which involve the gifts of people whose potential as contributors to worship is generally ignored. When a congregation is open to new possibilities and is able to welcome contributions from unexpected sources, all sorts of gifts become apparent. The task of helping people to be receptive like this is also part of the vocation of a pastor. Consider these possibilities:

(*a*) *Recorded music.* What theological, historical or liturgical reasons are there for thinking that only live music can lead us into the presence of God. (One might go on to question the almost universal assumption that only organ music can serve this purpose but that is another matter.) Some years ago at the British Council of Churches youth event 'Dayspring' it was apparent that people were arriving early for both morning and evening prayers and that they often stayed after the services were over to listen to the music, which on most occasions was recorded. Very few churches are equipped at present to provide this facility, but could not the gifts of our hi-fi enthusiasts be so used in the service of God.

(*b*) *The spoken word.* No act of worship worthy of the name will lack at least one reading from the Holy Scriptures. Yet are there not other words which might ennoble the human spirit and impart a sense of wonder, majesty and holy fear? In our congregations there will be those who love and are familiar with the treasures of our literature, and there will be some who can read aloud in such a way as to inspire others. Cannot these gifts be used to the glory of God?

(c) *Visuals*. I am haunted by the lady who became increasingly deaf and eventually left her own church because, she said, 'There's nothing in its services to appeal to the eye'. Yet there are creative people in our congregations who could lead others to worship through their eyes. Our trouble is that we seem to have to choose between all or nothing; if we accept a piece of sculpture or a tapestry for the church it has to be on display the whole time or someone takes offence. What I have in mind is that people should lend items for one service only, or perhaps a short season. One of the members of the congregation to which I belong has a gift for collage. At certain seasons of the year the church is filled with banners illustrating aspects of the theme of the day. Were they to be on display the whole year round their impact would soon be lost. As a way of highlighting a special occasion their use is splendid. In a similar way the work of woodcarvers, embroiderers, weavers, photographers, artists, sculptors and creative people in all kinds of media, might become a means of grace. We accept the skills of the flower arranger, why not also the potter, the welder, or the glass blower?

(d) *Live music*. We accept the offering of singers, but we do so only within very narrowly defined limits. We accept those who can sing in congregations and those who can sing in choirs of about twelve to twenty people and are willing to accept the boundaries of the organist's taste. These probably extend from the birth of Handel to the death of Stainer but no further. But we also need to accept the gifts of those who sing best on their own, or with two or three others. We have to welcome those who are more likely to be found at the Rainbow Theatre or the Hammersmith Odeon than at the Festival Hall. We have to ask ourselves why there is so little in our worship of the music that inspires young people in their tens of thousands at Taizé or the Greenbelt Festival. We should make a good start doing away with the idea of a 'church choir' with all the overtones of status and exclusivity that implies and thinking instead of church musical resources which, in the case of a particularly fortunate church, might take the form of a number of choirs of all shapes and sizes, a folk group, a rock group, a steel band, together with assorted soloists. It goes without saying that the pastor who can cope with this range of artistic temperament will be a man of God indeed.

(e) *Dance*. Dance is a minority taste and should be used sparingly. However, some people do communicate very well with their bodies and there may be more in future, thanks to the interest in dance drama being shown in many schools. However, I do not include as a resource for public worship what is commonly called 'dancing in the Spirit' which too easily becomes self-indulgent and should be confined to private devotion.

(f) *Drama*. While so many churches have drama societies that are not unwilling to mount a 'religious play' when they can find a good one, our general inability to use drama as a natural ingredient of worship is surprising. Yet dramatic episodes can contribute greatly to a service, not least in bringing out the humour in the NT, and scripts are available from a variety of sources for those without the resources to devise their own. (See for example, *Time to Act* (Hodder & Stoughton, £1·25), and material from Christian Aid and the Bible Society. Write also to RADIUS, the Religious Drama Society of Great Britain, at St Paul's Church, Covent Garden, Bedford Street, London WC2E 9ED. The spring 1982 issue of AIM published by the Methodist Home Mission Division lists other sources of dramatic material.)

(g) *Other liturgical material*. All over the world new

forms of worship are being evolved, new prayers written, new music sung. Part of the pastor's task is to keep track of at least some of it. Events like a general assembly of the World Council of Churches yield a veritable mine of liturgical resources as do centres of pilgrimage like Iona, Corymeela and Taizé. These resources are not only valuable in themselves but enable congregations to have a real sense of sharing in a world-wide worshipping family.

Two words of warning in conclusion. New forms of worship must arise out of the discovery by the congregation that they have more gifts to offer in worship than they had previously supposed. The purpose of this article has been to suggest some of the gifts we might look for. It is not the new forms themselves that bring worship to life but the process of discovery. Many of the ideas suggested will be beyond the resources of some congregations, but they may furnish yet other ideas once the process of discovery has begun. New forms should never be imposed and hardly ever imported. We must begin with our people, sharing with them in order that together we may discover and release those gifts which may enable the whole community to become more aware of the reality of God and to respond to him more joyfully and completely.

The second warning is that it is all very hard work. It is much easier to keep worship to ourselves than to share it with others, much less arduous to do things for people than to engage with them. If we take seriously our role as creators and initiators rather than leaders and performers it will make new demands upon our time, upon our gifts, and especially upon our nerves. We shall nevertheless have a more truly pastoral ministry, being shepherds after the pattern of Jesus who did not come to do for us what we should be doing ourselves but to enable us to be one with him in fellowship with God the father.

# Preparing the Weekly Sermon

EDMUND S. P. JONES, B.A., B.D., Ph.D.
Washington, D.C.

A MINISTER received a query from the Civil Defence Unit asking how many people could be accommodated in the church in the event of an attack: 'I don't rightly know', he replied, 'but we sleep 300 comfortably every Sunday'. He understood all too well the enormous demands made upon a man who is expected to preach every week to the same congregation with interest, sensitivity and insight. The purpose of this chapter is to indicate some practical ways in which the burden may be eased and a measure of confidence assured as the week-end draws near.

Great preachers like great orators are few and far between. But the art of speaking effectively can be learned by even the least articulate. Moses' ministry may have started off with the lament, 'I have never been a man of ready speech' (Ex $4^{10}$) but he became the voice of a new people. As Wm. James said: 'Let no youth have any anxiety about the upshot of his education. If he keeps faithfully busy he can find himself one of the competent ones of his generation.'

A sermon can't be cooked to order like a steak. It must have time to grow. So start off each term — a year is probably too long — by selecting and writing down the themes that you may like to tackle. At this stage, a week browsing in the library to find possible series and topics that interest and excite is probably the best week's work in the year. There's no use expecting it to be easy. However, it will not only subsequently reduce the anxiety curve by half and save hours wondering where to start but will repay tenfold in time saved. The selection should not be too rigid for there will be times of crisis when minds are unusually open to hear a word from God. Heaven forgive the man who treats his congregation to a dissertation on 'the Temple' when the village has just lost a fishing boat or the local factory has been closed and the workforce put on the dole! There is an immediate impact and interest which the well-chosen topical sermon can count on, and all good preaching should be authentically God's word at God's time. If the Bible is one source book the newspaper is certainly another.

Some series suggest themselves — the Ten Commandments, the Parables, the Apostles' Creed. Watch the Lord's Prayer and the Minor Prophets. The bones are there but many a minister has learned — too late — that it takes time for the meat to become succulent. Only the very brave or the very leisured announce a series without first having sketched out, even in a rudimentary way, the later parts of the series as well as the earlier.

The OT often provides a richer human starting point because it centres on personalities whereas the NT — particularly the latter part — is stronger on ideas and concepts. An excellent starter is A. S. Hopkinson: *Modern Man reads the Old Testament* (Hodder & Stoughton) which gives almost 200 brief, lively original introductions to biblical people and events. *The Living World of the Old Testament* by Bernhard Anderson (Longmans), and *Ancient Israel — its Life and Institutions* by R. de Vaux (Darton, Longman & Todd) provide good distilled scholarship for the busy practitioner with limited financial resources for library building.

A planned series of topics avoids the experience of a blank face staring down at a blank piece of paper. It's a starting point. There must also be a starting time. Never start preparing until you feel inspired — but make sure you feel inspired at 9.00 a.m. on Tuesday morning. A. J. Gossip tells how he met Christ and received his message as he turned the corner of the pulpit steps on Sunday, but presumably neither he nor God normally left it as late as that.

James S. Stewart started sermon preparation first thing on Tuesday morning. So did Leslie Weatherhead. Willie Barclay never wrote a sermon after Thursday. One suspects that an alarmingly high number of ministers fritter their mornings away and then are feverishly searching for a text on Saturday night. An exhausted preacher is not likely to be a relaxed and effective preacher the next day. So form the habit of starting on time and doing solid work each morning in the study.

Even with a disciplined schedule time is very limited. So set aside the first hour for homiletical reading not immediately related to Sunday and choose your books carefully. With the exception of Hans Küng's *On Being a Christian* (Collins) I generally find smaller books more helpful. Titles that come to mind include: *Mystery and Imagination* by R. P. C. Hanson (SPCK), *Cancer and the God of Love* by M. Thompson (SCM) and *New Light on Old Songs* by Kenneth Slack (SCM). Heavier reading that no minister can ignore for long includes: Bornkamm's *Jesus of Nazareth* (Hodder & Stoughton), Schweizer's *Jesus* (SCM), J. A. Baker's *The Foolishness of God* (Fontana) — not forgetting Moltmann. Dorothee Sölle's book *Suffering* (Darton, Longman & Todd) is an unusually sensitive theological discussion of a difficult subject. Rosemary Ruether's book: *Mary — the Feminine Face of the Church* (SCM) gives a fresh touch for the Mothers Day sermon, and Martin Hengel's books have lots of interesting human touches.

Never read without marking or making notes. Better still, take the trouble to start a scrap-book of facts, quotations, etc. Its value will geometrically increase every year and it is one of the best safety nets for the week you were out of town or not well. It isn't enough to read. You must be able quickly to locate material and recall things read a long time ago. Biography of all kinds is enjoyable and a fruitful source of illustration and insight. D. L. Moody, pre-eminent among a generation of evangelists who mastered the art of speaking without electronic assistance and television techniques tells how he prepared his addresses:

> When I choose a subject, I write the name of it on the outside of a large envelope. I have many such envelopes. If, when I am reading, I meet a good thing on any subject I am to speak on, I slip it right into the right envelope. . . . Perhaps I let it lie there for a year or more. When I want a new sermon, I take everything that has been accumulating. Between what I find there and the results of my own study, I have material enough.

The successful and lively preacher is one who has a 'barrel' in front of him as well as behind him.

Now it is time for the actual sermon preparation. Techniques differ and each individual must find what suits him. Leslie Weatherhead wrote a full script and then revised it three or four times before reducing it to notes for delivery. A good plan is to take a page of foolscap paper and note down every thought, idea, illustration, question and association. As Richard Whately said, 'Preach not because you have to say something but because you have something to say'. The best sermons will be those that come from your own thinking and feeling rather than compiled from other people's work. Allow your mind to reflect on the subject from as many different perspectives as possible. The more your own interest is kindled the more likely the theme will interest those who listen. Equally, the longer you have lived with the topic, even if only reflecting on it when walking in the evening or travelling by train or linking it with something viewed on television, the more likely it will have gripped your interest and stimulated your imagination. Much of the material may be revised or even discarded but it is the remainder that will give the fresh stamp of your personality to an old subject.

From there move to books, articles, scrap-book and briefly a commentary. The latter may occasionally prevent an embarrassing mistake but very few are of direct help in preaching. Learn to dip into books especially encyclopedias for background information. Cultivate an eye for human interest stories from newspapers. It will be an original start to a sermon on the 'Stilling of the Storm' if you remembered to file the report some years back of an American woman who sued God for negligence over the weather!

Never be afraid to tell people in non-technical language what the theologians are talking about. The pulpit is not here to protect the pew but to share with it, and many ministers deplorably underestimate the intelligence and spiritual search of their congregations. They'll be far more interested as well as better informed Christians if instead of denouncing Mariolatry they know how that strand of piety started. Is it carelessness, incompetency or fear that has prevented the churchgoer from learning such simple theological facts as how the Bible was written, when the Church started to pray directly to Christ, or what were the issues in 'The Myth of God Incarnate' debate?

An important part of understanding literature is to read literature. An important part of sermon preparation is to read sermons — less for content, more for style and approach. Eric Routley's *Saul Among the Prophets* (Epworth) contains the best modern series of sermons on the patriarchs. Helmut Thielicke's *How the World Began* (Clarke) shows that good expository preaching can also be intensely human. Archie Hunter's *Design for Life* (SCM) has clarity and vigour as well as scholarship. Harry A. Williams *The True Wilderness* (Constable) remains a classic. Both books of sermons from Great St Mary's University Church are worth having, and though the current weekly printed sermons are primarily for undergraduates they can be a useful source of topics. A cheque for £5 to the Secretary, Great St Mary's, Cambridge, will bring morning and evening sermons during term-time.

Avoid like the plague the common practice of starting by announcing a text — some men do it twice on the assumption that everyone is deaf or already falling asleep! There are infinitely more interesting ways of introducing a subject. The first few words are often the hardest to write. Frequently they are the most important. Look at Colin Morris' *Get Through Till Nightfall* (Collins) for immediately interesting openings to religious questions. Peggy Makin's *Thoughts, Prayers, Reflections* (BBC) commences with the simple human sentence about 'Red Letter Days', or 'Quarrels', or 'Secret Love' which immediately rings true for most people. Indeed the BBC's series 'Thought for the Day' should be obligatory reading for every preacher who wants to speak simply and effectively to people.

The main difficulty in all sermon-preparation is not what to say but how to say it. A good sermon invariably has three qualities. It is simple. It is concrete. It is relevant.

Despite what is said about theology as an important part of good preaching the sermons which will undoubtedly be most satisfying will be those which try to help with ordinary problems. That makes the greatest demands on sensitivity, honesty and perception. An older book such as Karl Olsson's *Seven Sins and Seven Virtues* (Hodder &

Stoughton) is a good starter. *Our Rebel Emotions* (Hodder & Stoughton) by Bernard Mobbs is a more conservative approach but less stimulating and perceptive. In contrast Monica Furlong's *Christian Uncertainties* (Hodder & Stoughton) like most of her books combines Christian conviction with a salutary dose of sound commonsense.

Listen to Alastair Cooke's 'Letter from America'. Every sentence is immediately understandable yet never shallow. John Wesley, who preached in an age which had not been bewitched by the television screen, would go over his sermon again and again crossing out every word not immediately comprehensible to the ordinary person. That kind of time and care is a mark of the professional who really knows the trouble that has to be taken to communicate well.

By 'concreteness' is meant expressing the scriptural themes in terms of people rather than principles, events rather than doctrine. The Parable of the Talents will be far more interesting if the minister has first of all taken the time to find out how Christ's hearers would have invested surplus cash and what the bank-rate was in the first century Palestine. Paul the theologian deals largely in concepts, analogies and rules. Jesus the Teacher expresses the most profound theological truths in stories about people which are arresting because they are real and immediately recognizable.

The story is still one of the most effective vehicles for preaching. In an age when many congregations are scripturally illiterate most preachers need to re-tell the great biblical stories far more often. Done with lively imagination, vividness of phrase, and occasional touches of humour people never grow tired of the great stories and they form an invaluable link between the generations. Unless you have a natural flair for story-telling study

Kossoff's *Bible Stories* or some such book for clues to the art.

Closely allied to both simplicity and humanity is relevance. Start off talking about Moses going up Mount Nebo to view the Promised Land though he would never set foot in it, and you run the risk of losing all but the most attentive. So why not start a sermon on disappointment by relating the true story of the athlete who trained intensely for the Moscow Olympics, was disqualified in the preliminary heats for foot-faulting, and left the arena in tears. The way is then open to talk about the disappointments we all experience in our jobs, or in our marriages, or in the way the children turn out. By the time we reach Moses he is no longer a remote Semitic figure but one of us and his God close to us too.

As I write brother Billy is embarrassing President Carter, Richard Nixon had his brother Donald, Lincoln's wife was alleged to be a southern spy, and almost every family has at least one black sheep whom the other members try to keep hidden. So the way opens for a true grasp of the bewilderment of the elder brother in the Prodigal Son parable. The Bible becomes fascinating when it no longer is treated as a collection of texts, but as a look at how people coped with the feelings of frustration, hope, loneliness and fear of death which are common to all of us.

Knox Little, Canon at Canterbury Cathedral, used to say that a preacher never grasped the full message in a sermon until he had delivered it six times. It is one thing to write a sermon. It is another to feel it deep within, and sense the rise and fall of its moods and pattern. The latter is that which gives it the personality and persuasion of the speaker. So write as you would speak. Rehearse it many times until the literary quality gives way to the much more direct and taut oral communication. We should study how to put the sermon over effectively as well as what to include in its content. We should practise delivery with the same dedication as an actor because preaching can still change peoples lives. Just because the Word takes on human garb in our halting and inadequate utterance we dare not minimize the hard toil and discipline which the craft requires. To be thoroughly professional is to avoid the biting wit of Mark Twain who once commented on an acquaintance: 'He charged nothing for his preaching — and it was worth it too'.

# Family Services?

KENNETH STEVENSON
Manchester

EVERY church has got its conversation-stopper, and when it comes to worship there are many. 'Are you interested in liturgy?' asked the old lady of Dean Inge; 'No, Madam, neither do I collect stamps'. It's obvious that when it comes to matters of worship, churches put up their defence-barriers even more quickly than they do in other areas of its life. A theologian can make any number of blunders, but the liturgist cannot afford to, or if he does, the consequences of that blunder are more far-reaching than someone's inaccurate exegesis of a Pauline epistle from the pulpit.

When I say 'liturgist' perhaps I ought to define my terms. I enjoy some Scandinavian ancestry, and delight in the fact that in Danish, 'liturgist' is still a word commonly used of the 'celebrant', 'president', 'officiating minister'. Whether you're a High Anglican or a Free Evangelical, the powers of discretion that lie in the lap of those responsible for the conduct of public worship are great indeed. These powers need to be used creatively, and nowhere more so than in the kind of worship which many of us call 'Family Services'.

Many people sneer at them, and some of the sneerers are those who are not particularly interested in forms of worship anyway. I doubt that what I have to say here (or in my recent book[1]) will convince them. What I am concerned about is that at least we recognize why Family Services are with us, what they are, and how they can be compiled in such a way that they are part of the mainstream of local church-life, and not a fringe-benefit.

Much of what I am going to say is based on some Anglican parochial experience in Lincolnshire, in several quite different settings, including the local Methodist chapel. Readers who are not part of either of these traditions will, I hope, bear with me; I'm not trying to do a piece of Anglican triumphalism ('We've just discovered this need, here it is, you'd better *all* see it now'), particularly as the composition of evangelistic non-eucharistic services is not something in which the Church of England has experience comparable to the great English Dissenting communities.

Family Services are the response to a widely-felt need in many churches where the old Victorian legacy of dividing the church-community into many different groupings is being adapted, in favour of a truly corporate style of worship, where the whole age-range meets, and contributes in different ways. This is, if you like, the liturgical answer to The International Year of the Child, which was a fruitful year in which many began to realize that children are not small-adults, but are people in their own right, with their own spirituality, and their own vital contribution to what the rest of us do. Colin Davis once admitted that he wished he felt the same love towards Elgar's music he knew before he went through the agonizing critical stage of his student days; he didn't want to become child-ish but he wanted to be child-*like* . . . and this is a difference that Christians have talked about for a long time without actually understanding particularly acutely.

The other main reason for Family Services is the need to have an outreach to the parents, relatives and friends of children and teenagers who are associated with week-day (and Sunday) activities of local congregations. By this I mean (though not exclusively) organizations like Sunday Clubs. Many are the churches that are bursting at the seams with people in those age-groups, but little is done to attract parents. I know of one church where parents have been brought into fellowship, and many parsons know what stimulating adult-confirmation candidates they can be. Often they have been baptized in infancy, went to a bit of Sunday-School, and then dropped out because there was little to meet their needs. There is no reason why there should not be a strategy — not to make people feel 'got at', but to provide them with an atmosphere in which they can feel at home, in which they won't feel guilty about having 'lapsed', in which they can grow; here perhaps they can be presented with a celebration of Christian faith which does not demand from them the eucharistic fellowship which is initially too much for them.

This last point is particularly appropriate for Anglicans, because the growth of the 'Parish Communion' Movement and the decline of big, popular Evensongs have together meant that there have rarely been services for 'the many' that are not eucharistic, or, if there were, they consisted of a complex series of liturgical ingredients, like Mattins and Evensong. 'Folk-religion' is still around, but you can no longer go into an Old Folks' Home and expect them all to know even some easy hymns by heart, let alone the Magnificat or the Apostles' Creed. There is certainly an element of the 'liturgy of the catechumenate' about these celebrations, in which genuinely Christian worship takes place, but in an adapted form, through which they can be introduced to the basics of the Christian life.

Here, I am not arguing for a scheme of Family Service quite disconnected from the eucharistic worship of the congregation; if anything, the reverse. Perhaps some people were surprised at just how 'eucharistic' my little book is. I still think that the authentic Christian celebration is the baptismal eucharist, with its essential features of what Karl

Barth called *Wort* and *Antwort* ('Word' and 'Response'); and any eucharist, in its two main parts (supremely with baptism in the first part), embodies these two features of the Christian life. How, then, can Family Services point to the eucharist? The main answer to this question is in a strategy which includes some eucharistic material in the service and also in having a eucharist in the service a few times in each year. Thus, if your Family Service occurs every month, you may consider holding a eucharist at it once a quarter, or perhaps just twice a year. If you do, the service will need careful presentation and adaptation, and (in my own opinion) *stretching* the present official rites rather than using them as they are.

How, then, can these services be linked with the rest of the congregation's life? There are many places in which the Family Service takes place very infrequently, and is really a sop to the Sunday School teachers and the Curate, in order to leave the Vicar with the 'real' job of looking after the Sung Eucharist There are many ways, and they are not just 'techniques' to be 'used' with ecclesiastical 'slickness'. (I would myself warn anyone off a Family Service programme unless there is a real commitment to its principles and an awareness of its context.) One way is to link the theme of the service with the work of the Junior Church groups in the Sundays before-hand, including the Youth Club; another way is to have some notes or study-material for congregational house-groups in the weeks after. But all this needs careful planning and good co-ordination. Thus, a service for May on the theme of 'work' could well bring together some projects from the Junior Clubs in the weeks before, and lead into a whole range of discussion in the house-meetings in the weeks after about local unemployment and the theology of 'work' and 'leisure', and the value of being human and its essential meaning in the image of God.

Other ways relate to the compilation of the service itself, for here there are many different ingredients, one of which is *Word*. I discovered that one of the best ways to train people in the principles of good worship is to get them to help plan and 'perform'; and the whole process pays dividends in getting their own understanding to develop. Thus, a well-prepared dialogue-sermon (when they are badly-prepared they ramble on) has the effect of sharpening people's concentration, so that sidesmen at the back of church notice how heads turn from one lectern to another, like a good day at Wimbledon. Similarly, people feel involved when a well-presented piece of drama is performed on stage-blocks, or a mime, accompanied by reading, or music, or both. The old psychology of the Greek stage certainly holds true; involvement can be at all levels of the human personality, not just the cerebral. This brings me on to make another point; dramatic-reading and dramatic-presentations belong naturally to the 'Word' aspect of the service, but it should not be allowed to dominate over the others, such as 'Prayer' and 'Praise'. Far too often, parsons abuse the Family Service, and unnecessarily offend big congregations by a well-intentioned but quite inappropriate lengthy harangue, such as, 'you should come to church *every* Sunday'. Another danger is the temptation, particularly rife among amateur educationalists in the cloth, to 'explain' everything — including drama. There really is no need to explain it, otherwise, what is the point of performing it? Have a discussion afterwards for those who want to, or some sort of 'come-back'; but 'introductions' (the bane of modern liturgy — including the new Roman mass) should be avoided, and only used when really necessary, and then should be very carefully planned.

*Praise* can vary in style. You need to ask yourself 'what sort of hymn should we start with?', and it should usually be something well-known, since a little-known hymn at the beginning of a Family Service can kill the celebration stone-dead. Sometimes organists with high principles need some taming to come down to a mortal level in this regard Generally speaking, hymns should be chosen for their content, though we all fall into the trap occasionally of chosing them for their tunes; but a service should begin with a hymn of adoration, continue with hymns of reflection (between the readings) and devotion (near the intercessions), and conclude with a hymn of 'resolve'. Not every hymn falls into one of these categories, and of course there are exceptions. Another point worth making is that choirs can be used to sing special pieces that do fit into the theme of the service, and, of course, this is more likely to fit in with the entire enterprise if there are good relations between the choir and the rest of the congregation. But frequently, some group will want to teach the congregation something new and this can raise problems. Should there be a 'rehearsal' before the service actually starts, or should the 'teach-in' take place during the service itself? Opinions vary on this one, and you may find different solutions working on different occasions. Modern hymns do need to be introduced, since we are living through an explosion in hymn-writing, and the best way to test them is to try them out; it is as destructive to judge a hymn from reading its text and humming through its tune as it is to assess a new liturgy simply be reading through the libretto. By 'try out' you should mean actually doing it, and risking it. But remember that not everyone is musical, and for far too long we have neglected prose-psalmody and choric speech, fine material for which can be found in some of the biblical canticles in the new Roman Divine Office.

*Prayer* is the third main ingredient, and it should take a natural place in the order of service. Not every Family

Service needs to have all the four traditional kinds,
adoration, confession, thanksgiving and supplication, but
these four do have a real logic about them; we adore God in
response to the possibility of worshipping him; we confess
our inadequacy because we feel it as a result of adoring him;
we give thanks because we are forgiven; and as a result of
giving thanks, we pray for certain specific things, so that we
may go out and serve the world. Many Family Services
degenerate into a 'hymn-sandwich', and some even become
'prayer-sandwiches', with different kinds of prayer pep-
pered over the main dish (hymnody), to make the entirety
slightly more appetising. The traditional collect for the day
is frequently a good prayer to associate closely with the
readings; forms of confession exist in both hymnody and
psalmody, as well as the official forms of service;
intercession is a good feature to share round members of
the congregation, particularly those who have the natural
gift of prayer-writing. When it comes to thanksgiving, it
could well be that you can use one or other of the so-called
'dry eucharistic prayers' in the Methodist Service Book (or
the first part of the official eucharistic prayers in the ASB),
thereby introducing the congregation to one important
feature of liturgical worship which will familiarize them
with the eucharistic rite. Anglicans (and others) might take
the opportunity of using the Sanctus (in the official or
metrical versions) after these Thanksgivings. But local
talent may exist for a new style of language, as in the
*Rodborough Bede-Book,* or the approach taken in the
works of Huub Oosterhuis or Alan Gaunt. It seems a pity if
a service which is specially composed should repeat
ecclesiastical conventions, particularly as those eras in the
past which we can now identify as particularly creative in
liturgical development (e.g. fourth-century Syria, eighth-
century Gaul, sixteenth-century Germany) were ones which

encouraged local improvisation in the quest for new styles and forms and theological insights.

In conclusion, let me add a word or two of warning, which may sound cautious, but is not meant to; beware lest one of the three main ingredients dominates at the expense of the other two. Too much praise makes it a sing-song (and nothing more); too much word makes it unbearably 'preachy'; and too much prayer will rob the service of its bite. As in any act of worship, the right balance between these ingredients keeps the service healthy, wholesome, coherent; and I do recognize that they overlap, even though they are distinct. Another *caveat* is to prepare sufficiently beforehand so that everything happens naturally. Whether you have lots of movement, ceremonial or whatever you like to call it, you do need to rehearse what is to be done by the leaders, who may become a good team in time, and comprise a good cross-section of the whole congregation. This is not in order to make the barrier between 'audience' and 'actors' all the greater, but rather to break it down. Well-rehearsed movement looks more natural and less mannered than a shambles which lacks meaning (or indeed an effete sanctuary-manoeuvre that doesn't seem to get anywhere). Let me end on a simple but profound note: liturgy, whatever its style and content is the educational matrix of the church; all our teaching and learning and training lacks digestion until it becomes part of our worship of the Lord who so often comes to make all things new in the most surprising ways.

---

[1] *Family Services* (SPCK [1981]).

# Baptism for the Asking

WILLIAM D. HORTON, M.A.
Sevenoaks

THE purpose of this article is not to argue the case for infant, as against believers', baptism. That issue has been well debated in recent years and most pastors are clear where they stand on the matter. Our present concern is with the dilemma faced by those pastors who are prepared to justify and practise infant baptism for the children of Christian, church-going parents, but who are very unhappy when asked to baptize the children of non-believers. When a couple who, apparently, have no links with any church stand on his doorstep and ask him to 'do' their baby (in all probability, 'next Sunday'!) what is the pastor to say? When, in conversation, the parents betray a woeful ignorance of the Christian faith, the Christian way of life and the significance of Christian baptism, ought he to grant or withhold the sacrament? This article, while recognizing the dilemma, argues the case for *never* refusing baptism to any baby, on the grounds that 'baptism for the asking' is both theologically and pastorally right; it concludes with a paragraph about the ordering of the baptismal service.

## Theological Issues

The theological issues relate to the meaning of baptism, the place of children in the church and the extent to which faith is essential for a valid sacrament. But these can only be discussed, adequately, in the context of the gospel as a whole; our Christian belief and practice derive from (and must reflect) what is 'given' in our message. A brief statement about the nature of the gospel, therefore, must come first.

1. The gospel proclaims that, in the life, death and resurrection of Jesus, God has declared his love for mankind and his purposes for the world; that God has done everything needful for man's salvation, in forgiving the past, effecting reconciliation in the present and promising new life for the future; that God invites all men to receive the benefits of salvation by sharing in a covenant relationship with his Son; that God's action in Christ is not restricted to individuals of a particular time or place, but is 'crucial' for the whole cosmos and for all time. It follows, therefore, that all is of God and all is of grace; that God claims everyone, everything, everywhere, for himself; that no limit of any description can be placed on his love and in that love, made flesh in Christ, all things find their meaning and fulfilment. This summary of the gospel (inevitably incomplete and selective) is the broad, sweeping backcloth against which the more specific issues must now be considered.

2. The meaning of baptism. To regard baptism simply as the means by which a person (adult or infant) joins the Christian church is to over-stress its human, matter-of-fact, aspect and under-value it as a holy sacrament. Even to regard it just as the initiation into the Christian *faith* is to miss its primary significance as a gospel 'mystery' which man can neither fully understand nor bring about. Baptism is the way of entry into the Christian faith and into the church only because it is, first of all, baptism 'into Christ'. In baptism, an ordinary human being who is, by nature, part of a sinful world becomes 'engrafted' (cf. the Westminster Confession) into God's saving activity and, in Christ, is promised a new nature as a child of God; a fallen creature of space and time is lifted up in the ground-swell of

God's eternal purposes for creation and incorporated into that spiritual kingdom where his sinfulness can be dealt with and his true destiny fulfilled (Rom $6^{3-11}$). Baptism is the gospel in action, declaring what God has done and is doing, today; it stems only from God's initiative in Christ; it is of significance only as an affirmation of God's claim upon every human life and as an expression of his love freely given for all mankind. The water and the three-fold name sparkle with the life of God, the great Redeemer.

If this understanding of baptism expresses the gospel, can the sacrament rightly be refused to any child? Of course it can't To deny *anyone* the opportunity of being included (and of being *seen* to be included) in God's redemptive activity is to set human limits to the power of the Holy Spirit. To make *anything* the *sine qua non* of baptism is to set a human price-tag on what God offers 'gratis' and to erect barriers against God's all-embracing love. Conversely, to grant baptism whenever it is requested is to respond to God's initiative in coming 'to seek and to save the lost', to proclaim the supreme worth of every individual in God's sight and to act in harmony with Christ who, without screening the parents, welcomed all the children who were brought to him. Baptism only for those who have the right credentials is hardly worth having. It reduces the sacrament to the level of 'joining the club' and destroys rather than preserves its significance. Only baptism for all who ask for it is worthy of Christ and the gospel.

3. The place of children in the church. Jesus leaves us in no doubt about the place of children in God's *kingdom*. Children are the very fabric of that kingdom and lead the way into it; all who receive a child in Christ's name receive both Christ and God himself, while those who cause a child to stumble in life face the direst penalties (Mk $9^{35-37, \ 42}$, $10^{13-16}$). In none of this is there any indication that Jesus

ever qualified his statements about children. He never made
the faith, the understanding or the good character of the
parents a condition of his acceptance of their child. This
was not because he was a starry-eyed sentimentalist where
children were concerned, but because he realized that, *as
children,* they occupied a special place in the economy of
God's kingdom; their trustful nature, their sense of
complete dependence, their response to love, their openness
to life and spiritual realities were the key which unlocked
the secrets of that kingdom. For Christ, to welcome *any*
child was to demonstrate the greatness of the least, to
proclaim the gospel that God's love is freely and uncon-
·ditionally offered to all.

Although the visible church is not to be equated with the
kingdom of God, if it is to conform to the gospel it must
reflect the values of that kingdom rather than those of the
world. Whereas secular society tends to regard children as
potential adults and directs their 'up-bringing' towards the
goal of their majority when they can share fully in the
responsibilities and privileges of the adult (real?) world, the
church must recognize that children don't have to become
responsible adults to be fully part of God's family;
responsible adults have to become children! Children are
not 'the church of tomorrow', they are, by right, the church
of today and in the kingdom-centred church the goal of the
Christian life must always be childlikeness.

In this context, to baptize only the children of Christian,
church-going parents is to take an adult point of view. It is
to set a higher value on the standing of the parents than of
the children and, consequently, to deny many children
(through no fault of their own) their right to receive the
blessings of the sacrament. It is also to imply that what
children may become is more important than what they are
now, and that unless there is a likelihood that the goal of

Christian adulthood will be reached (via a Christian up-bringing) baptism is meaningless. Baptism for the asking, however, recognizes the rightful place of children in the church. It proclaims that every child, as a child, belongs to God's kingdom, today; that God demands nothing (not even Christian parents) from children and offers everything, through grace, here and now.

4. How far is faith essential for a valid baptism? Because baptism is firstly God's action in claiming a child for himself, there is a divinely objective element in the sacrament which doesn't depend on human faith for its presence. The faithfulness of God is prior to the faith of man; God is never at our mercy through our lack of faith. However! If the blessings of baptism are to be *appropriated* by the human partners to it, then faith in God's saving activity in the sacrament is indispensable; that God's initiative requires man's response is always a corollary of the gospel. Pastors who refuse to baptize the children of non-Christian parents argue that the absence of parental faith makes nonsense of the rite. How can a baptism be valid (they say) if the persons most intimately concerned in it have no belief in the Christian truths it proclaims and no living experience, themselves, of God's love which they promise to make real to their child? God loves every child, anyway, so what does baptism add to the situation if the response of parental faith is not there?

Such criticisms would carry more weight if baptism were a service of dedication rather than a sacrament. Clearly, unbelievers can't play their part, adequately, in a dedicatory rite which involves the dedicators as much as, if not more than, the one dedicated. But baptism is *not* simply a dedication, as this article has attempted to show. Nor is it true that the only faith required for a valid infant baptism is that of the parents; the church, an essential partner in the baptism must exercise faith; the godparents, or sponsors, must be people of faith (if they're not, then their role *is* meaningless). Who dare say that, when a church really believes in the gospel and in the efficacy of Christ's saving work, the baptism of any child is pointless? The biblical evidence is that vicarious faith opens a door through which Christ can act, with power, in the lives of others (Mk $2^5$, Lk $7^{9-10}$).

To focus the issue, now, on the parents: is it right to regard any parents who request baptism for their child as entirely faith-less? Some parents may have only the haziest understanding of Christian belief and of what it means to live a fully Christian life but, at least, they believe that the sacrament offers something they want for their baby and, prompted by the Holy Spirit, they pluck up courage to ask for it. Surely, this is an act of faith in itself. Their request may be grounded in traditional religious observances and current social values, but they certainly don't dismiss baptism as irrelevant or unnecessary (as atheists would); their faith may be on the borderline of superstition, like that of the woman who only touched the hem of Christ's garment to be healed, but who is to say that it's not sufficient for the Saviour? If complete faith and perfect understanding are required of parents, who dare bring any child for holy baptism?

## Pastoral Considerations

The pastoral implications of allowing or denying baptism to the children of non-Christian parents must now be examined. Here, as in the theological debate, the arguments are strongly in favour of baptizing every child for whom baptism is sought. There are two main issues: the place of baptism in the church's mission and the nature of the pastor's responsibilities, in baptism.

The church is aware that its mission is to the world but it is not always sure how to exercise that mission effectively. How is the gulf between the church and the world to be bridged and God's claim asserted over the whole of human life? Baptism for the 'other sheep' of Christ's flock can contribute to an answer. No one, today, would advocate the pastor going out into the highways and by-ways to thrust baptism on all and sundry (as the Anglican incumbent was, at one time, expected to do and as the term 'indiscriminate baptism' might suggest). But where baptism is *requested,* the pastor is given free entry into a non-Christian home which, otherwise, might be closed to him. Provided the church fulfils its baptismal responsibilities, and the pastor, cradle-roll secretary, Sunday School staff and other caring Christians maintain contact with the family, the relationship established at the baptism can be strengthened, over the years, and the door kept open. Such a sensitive, pastoral ministry recognizes that God has a habit of coming to people (as he did to Mary and Joseph) in their children; it seizes the evangelical opportunities presented by the birth of a baby, fashioned in God's image, to challenge the parents.

If, however, baptism is refused to a child, a door is closed. Parents who are told that their baby can't be baptized because they themselves haven't the right qualifications are bound to feel confused and angry at being rebuffed. They will harbour resentment that a community which preaches God's love for the world has rejected their child who means 'all the world' to them; their hesitating attempt to make a link with the church having failed, they are not likely to respond favourably if the church, on some future occasion, seeks to win a commitment from them.

The other pastoral issue concerns the nature and extent of the pastor's responsibilities. These responsibilities need to be defined before deciding whether the pastor who restricts baptism to the children of Christian parents, or the pastor who welcomes all-comers, fulfils them better. They begin as soon as baptism is requested; just to fix a date for the service and to obtain the particulars for the certificate is not a fulfilment of them The pastor has a duty to explain to the parents, clearly and fully, the meaning of baptism, the nature of the promises they are required to make, the importance (in relation to the service) of a Christian up-bringing and how, with God's help and the support of the church, they can meet their parental obligations. Almost certainly, more than one interview with them will be necessary. At the baptism itself (see below), and afterwards, the pastor's responsibilities continue. In the name of the church, he must exercise a caring ministry in the home and ensure, to the best of his ability, that the baptismal vows are implemented; that the child grows up in a Christian environment; that he is led to a personal faith in Christ and that baptism is sealed in confirmation.

If these were the pastor's total responsibility in relation to baptism all would accept them and there would be little ground for distinguishing between one pastor and another. But there is a further responsibility. The pastor has a duty not to interfere with the parents' free exercise of *their* responsibilities. Having made clear to them the significance of Christian baptism, his task is then to ask the parents whether they accept baptism for their child, *on those terms*. Faced with this direct challenge some parents may withdraw their request; the majority will want the baptism to go ahead. In either case, at this point, the responsibility is properly theirs, not the pastor's. The pastor must not stand in the way of any parents entering into a religious commitment, on behalf of their child, provided its implications have been explained to them. Pastors who refuse to baptize children of other than Christian, church-going parents are in danger of pre-empting the work of the Holy Spirit. No pastor, however perceptive, can accurately gauge the parents' sincerity in making their vows; no pastor can be absolutely certain whether or not parents will keep their vows. These hidden things are between God and the parents, not the parents and the pastor, and God must be entrusted with them! It is the pastor who is prepared to baptize every child who fully acknowledges Christ's right to call whom he will, and the parents' right to respond to that call. Only he is prepared to recognize the possibility that, in the end, a miracle of grace may confound human probabilities. Only he, thereby, accepts the full responsibility of the pastoral office, in baptism.

## Ordering the Baptismal Service

If the pastor is convinced of the theological and pastoral 'rightness' of baptizing all for whom the sacrament is sought, he has a splendid opportunity to express his convictions in the Baptismal Service itself. That opportunity must not be missed by arranging the baptism for a time other than during the church's main act of worship. If (because the family 'doesn't belong to us') the baby is baptized in a cold and empty building, the church members are denied their rightful privilege and duty of being present, the parents are encouraged in the popular view that the service is only a private, child-naming ceremony from which they can quickly escape to the jollity of the christening party, and the pass is sold to those who argue that it is all little more than a traditional formality. The church which is always talking about its evangelistic task must be allowed to see that a family, not accustomed to church-going, has asked to come in. Let the church bells ring out in celebration A new life, with all its possibilities for good and evil, is being incorporated into God's saving purposes and welcomed into the family of Christ; the gospel of grace is being preached in word and deed; parents who, previously, have probably not thought much about religion are now recognizing that their child is a precious gift of God and are making a commitment on that child's behalf; so let all things be done joyfully, lovingly and meaningfully, within the Sunday worship. Above all, let the baptismal party feel 'at home' in the warmth and fellowship of a caring Christian community. If the service is seen for what it really is, its challenge and inspiration will be the foundations on which God can build his kingdom in human lives. If there is ever a possibility of *that* happening, no child should ever be denied baptism.

# Confirmation

WILLIAM D. HORTON, M.A.

Sevenoaks

AN issue can appear simple and straightforward until it is thought about carefully or proposed as the subject of an article! Then its complexities are revealed. The issue of confirmation is a case in point. Those who have grown up in the ordered life of the church may take for granted the Christian's progression from baptism through cradle-roll, Sunday school and confirmation class, to the confirmation service, first communion and the exercise of all the privileges and duties of church membership; they may see no difficulty in accepting this spiritual pilgrimage as entirely natural and comparable to a person's physical development from infancy to adulthood.

Problems only arise when the interaction between the different stages in this pilgrimage is examined and questions are asked about the precise relationship between confirmation and baptism, personal Christian experience and holy communion. This article raises these questions and discusses the theological problems as matters of the first importance; it then considers the secondary, practical problems concerning preparation for confirmation, the ordering of the confirmation service and the follow-up, afterwards.

## 1. *Theological problems*

First, what is the relationship between confirmation and infant baptism? The majority of church members (Nonconformists, at least) if confronted with this question, would probably say that confirmation marks the individual's reception into the 'full membership' of the church foreshadowed in the sacrament of baptism. At baptism a baby is offered to God and sealed with God's love to be brought up as a follower of Jesus Christ. At confirmation that act of faith bears fruit when, in thinking and acting for himself, the person takes his rightful place in the company of believers. But, if this understanding of the matter is accepted, the significance of baptism is misinterpreted (cf. 'Baptism for the Asking' (pp. 73-82). Baptism isn't primarily a dedication; it is a sacrament whereby a sinful human being is incorporated 'into Christ' and, thereby, incorporated into his body, the church. No membership can be more 'full' or complete than that and confirmation, in this respect, can add nothing to what has already been received. On the other hand, profession of faith has an essential part to play in church membership and, if baptism must not be undervalued as conveying only a partial or potential membership, neither must confirmation following baptism be dismissed as a superfluous irrelevancy.

How, then, is the baptism-confirmation relationship to be properly understood? It can only be understood in the context of divine grace. Baptism and confirmation are not two distinct forms of Christian initiation; they are not even two separate, though related, stages in Christian development. They are both facets of the same grace of God active in human life which, in different terms, express the one gospel of redemption. So membership in Christ and his church is one; it is fully expressed in baptism when a baby is 'engrafted' by the Spirit into Christ; it is fully expressed in confirmation when the same Spirit leads an adolescent or older person into a profession of faith in Christ's saving love. That profession of faith may indeed mark the individual's acceptance of vows made earlier, on his behalf, in baptism, but it is never simply a human response, a 'good work' which earns him entry into the church; it is a divine work, a work of grace enriching, renewing, strengthening, making personal, 'confirming' in the life of the individual all the blessings of God's kingdom equally available in baptism.

Theological matters cannot be considered in watertight compartments and, inevitably, the second question concerning confirmation has already been touched upon: what is the relationship between confirmation and a person's spiritual experience? It is popularly assumed that some time between baptism and confirmation (fulfilling the former and opening the door for the latter) a person comes to a saving knowledge of Christ which changes his life and vitalizes his faith. Without this experience, it is claimed, baptism remains incomplete and confirmation meaningless. This suggests, unfortunately, that countless youngsters who have been confirmed in their early or mid-teens (and often before this within the Roman Catholic Church) without having had a conscious spiritual experience bringing their faith alive, have subscribed to an empty form devoid of substance. But the work of God's Spirit in human life cannot be restricted to those times and events when the power of divine activity is subjectively felt and clearly observable. The biblical testimony is that all is of God; in him 'we live and move and have our being' (Acts $17^{28}$) and he is continually and creatively active in every part of human life. To God belong 'the slow watches of the night' as well as the stirring events of the day; the hidden, inward and almost imperceptible growth of spiritual awareness and response is as much his as the sudden, dramatic experience which transforms a person's life.

Because all is of God, the prime mover in confirmation (as in baptism) is the Holy Spirit. Our traditional use of the passive, 'being confirmed', rather than the active voice, indicates that the initiative is God's and not ours. Because all is of God, confirmation is *itself* an experience of the Spirit which doesn't depend for its validity on any prior experience; it *is* an experience, one which confirms God's work in a person's life and alone enables that person to profess faith in Christ and pledge loyalty to him as an act of will. This is not to deny the importance of the heart-warming experience which assures the Christian that he is a child of God, saved by Christ and indwelt by the Holy Spirit. It is just to affirm that such an experience is not the essential prerequisite of confirmation. Faith may indeed spark alive in the years between baptism and confirmation and so justify our tidy theological systems; it may spark alive only after confirmation, the rite having prepared the way for the subsequent experience; in the mystery of God's dealings with us it may not spark alive at all, although a person serve Christ faithfully all his days. Be these things as they may, confirmation stands in its own right as a gift of the Spirit, a spiritual experience to be received gratefully from the hands of him who bestows upon his children every good and perfect gift.

The third theological question concerns the relationship between confirmation and holy communion. Traditionally, first communion has followed confirmation, in the belief that taking communion implies a solemn Christian commitment for which preparation and understanding are required and which needs to be demonstrated by a public profession of faith in confirmation. Today, however, many churches celebrate 'family communion' where the children receive not just a blessing but the sacred elements themselves. Although the theology of the eucharist is not under consideration in this article, let it be said that any move which brings down the barriers at *the Lord's* table must be welcomed; sincerity of purpose and a *desire to receive* ought to be the only criteria for coming to communion, not moral standing, nor church membership, nor theological comprehension, nor age, nor confirmation.

But has the practice of allowing those not yet confirmed to take communion robbed confirmation of some of its meaning? In the sense that the rite is no longer the essential gateway into the richness of sacramental worship it has lost something, obviously. But in the sense that confirmation, after a person has become a regular communicant, is founded both on a fuller experience of the church's worship and on previous expressions of commitment in the sacrament, it can only be more surely and meaningfully based. Either way, it must not be forgotten that whatever precedes or follows it, confirmation stands on its own as an experience of God's Spirit. Therein lies its true value.

Space permits little more than a mention of other theological questions relating to confirmation; they must be left for the reader's consideration in the light of what has gone before. For instance, is confirmation really necessary after a person has made a profession of faith in believers' baptism? If an unbaptized adult seeks entry into the church, is baptism an essential precondition of confirmation? If a baptized infant later plays an active part in church life without ever having been confirmed, does he lack anything of significance in his discipleship? What implications has it for the meaning of the rite when a person who is confirmed (because it is 'the done thing') never darkens the church doors, afterwards? These questions betray our struggle to find a systematic theology with no loose ends; they mustn't encourage us to imagine that God is in any way limited by our systems, sacraments or ordinances. God can act outside all these things if he wills; his grace comes to each of us in a multitude of ways and his Spirit is never restricted to what we term 'the proper channels' in 'the right order'. None the less, Christian experience has shown that baptism, confirmation and eucharistic worship are among the richest gifts of his Spirit bestowed for our blessing and, therefore, never to be regarded as tiresome obligations or despised as 'merely' unimportant rites. Where confirmation is concerned, the Christian may receive confirmation of God's grace at many times and in many ways during his life and, by that same grace, may confirm his faith at many times and in many ways, but at one time the special way of confirmation is to be received as a gift of God, symbolic and determinative of all the others.

## 2. *Practical problems*

The first of these concerns the confirmation classes. No pastor would deny the need for careful preparation of confirmation candidates, over a considerable period, before the service. Many of those who seek confirmation (even those who have grown up in the Sunday School and the life of the worshipping community) will only have a hazy idea of things Christian; not only must the significance of confirmation be explained to them, they must also be given a basic understanding of Christianity. The pastor will realize the importance of this as he reflects that he may have no further opportunity (except through his sermons) of giving them systematic teaching. The content of the course will not present any problem. If he really is at a loss to know what to include, one of the many confirmation class manuals readily available in the religious bookshops will give him a scheme to work to (or adapt for his own requirements). The Christian's faith as outlined, say, in the Apostle's Creed, the growth of the church from its apostolic beginnings to the ecumenical movement (not forgetting the story of the denomination to which the local church belongs), Christian worship and sacraments, Christian devotion in prayer and Bible study, and Christian witness and service in the world will all have a place in the scheme.

The real problem facing the pastor in preparing confirmation candidates relates neither to need nor to content, but to method. Most of the candidates will be young people (what follows applies only to young people's groups; adult groups are not so frequently required and are easier to lead); although probably of similar social background, they will vary widely in intellectual ability and be at different stages of spiritual growth. How is the pastor to use the classes effectively so that the interest of every member is sustained and each of them is challenged by the gospel and built up in the faith? Older pastors, particularly, need to recognize that, in recent years, educational methods have changed radically and that it is self-defeating to use a form of teaching in the church that has long been out of use in the school. Youngsters who are accustomed to experimental learning, to 'projects' and activity, to the visual impact of television and the battery of other modern educational aids employed in the local school are neither inclined, nor able to sit still and listen to a forty-five minute lecture, especially if it is directed to those in the 'A' stream and is on a theological subject the relevance of which is not immediately clear. If the pastor requires this of them they will strain politeness to appear interested but, mentally, will switch off until the clock brings a merciful release.

How can the pastor tackle this problem? The following (tried) suggestions may help:—

(*a*) Let the main thrust of each session be the candidates' activity and the pastor's summing-up occupy no more than ten minutes at the end. Given imagination and effort, role-play, interviews, questionnaires, quizzes, paper and pencil work, discussions, games and many other activities can be used effectively in the teaching process. The local church can be explored and its features made the subject of a session on worship and the sacraments. Visits can be made to nearby places of interest (for example, Methodist groups in and around London can learn much of their church's history and ethos by visiting Wesley's Chapel, City Road, and the museum next door, together with the memorial to Wesley's conversion at the London Museum). Discovery not indoctrination will stimulate and challenge the youngsters, and they will learn!

(b) Let all the church's resources in people and equipment be fully utilized. It is a conceit to imagine that the pastor alone possesses everything necessary to lead the group. Others in the church, with special skills and spiritual gifts can lead certain sessions better than he, so let them be brought in to help! Local educational resource-centres can supply ideas for audio-visual aids and, often, hire out projectors, etc., if the church doesn't possess its own. There is a vast amount of suitable material waiting to be used.

(c) At the first meeting, let each candidate be given a foolscap envelope file in which to keep notes of the course and such booklets and other material it may be possible to provide. It is also helpful, then, to distribute a programme for the course, giving dates and places of meeting, the subjects and what is expected of the candidate concerning attendance, etc. At each subsequent session, work-sheets or topic-sheets outlining the theme, giving relevant Bible readings and suggesting questions to think about, can be provided for the file. In this way it is impressed upon the candidate that the church regards the classes as important and that, similarly, he or she must not approach them casually; and a personal file is built up for future reference.

The second practical problem (though it is more a question of fully seizing an opportunity than a problem) concerns the confirmation day itself. How can this be made a highlight of spiritual experience which the candidates will remember and draw strength from for the rest of their lives? Spiritual experiences are in God's gift, as we have noted, but prayer and preparation enable them to be received. Each meeting of the confirmation class should include a forward-looking prayer (led by the members in turn?). At the end of the course, each candidate should be interviewed, individually, and questioned about his or her sincerity in coming forward for confirmation. Each member of the congregation should be asked to pray, beforehand, for the candidates by name. Candidates, ministers, stewards and all taking part should be fully briefed about procedure, so that no uncertainty is allowed to detract from the service. Thus, everyone will approach the occasion in a spirit of expectancy. It is a happy gesture for representatives of the church (in addition to the pastor) to greet the candidates during the service and for one of them to present each candidate with a commemorative Bible or prayer book. Afterwards, over coffee in the church hall, the whole congregation can be invited to congratulate and welcome the newly-confirmed members; then, too, a group photograph can be taken as a reminder of the event. So, in these ways, confirmation is celebrated as a high point in the church's life.

However, when all has been faithfully said and done, and the candidates duly confirmed, one considerable problem remains. How can the newly-confirmed Christians be held within the active life of the church and enabled to grow in faith and love? How can the temptation to regard confirmation as the point of arrival rather than the spring-board for renewed growth in Christian understanding and commitment be resisted? The number of people who, once they are confirmed, begin to fall away from the church must not be allowed to increase! By writing a personal letter to each of the newly-confirmed members, in the week following the confirmation service, the pastor can outline the way ahead; he can indicate ways in which they can contribute to the church's work (if particular jobs can be given to them, so much the better). Although the pastor, himself, will need to give special care to the newly-confirmed members, particularly for the first year, certain of his more spiritually mature church members can be enlisted to share the pastoral responsibility so that the young people's links with the church are not only maintained but strengthened. On the occasion of the next confirmation service the young people can be invited to support the new group of candidates at it and renew their own vows of dedication. When, in the name of the church, the pastor has done all he can, one thing is still necessary: he must commit to God those for whom he is pastorally responsible, in the faith that he who is the initiator and confirmer of the spiritual life within us is also its perfecter and, in his good time, will bring to fruition all he has given.

# Weddings

WILLIAM D. HORTON, M.A.
Sevenoaks

'PLEASE can we see you about getting married?' In spite of the recent decline in the number of marriages contracted,[1] and notwithstanding that, of the smaller total, a higher proportion now takes place in the Register Office,[2] many couples still come to the pastor with this request. Not everybody regards marriage as an outmoded institution or Christian marriage as a superstition best forgotten! The pastor knows (and, often, expects) those who come to him from his own congregation; others are strangers who come because his church is nearest their home or has a reputation for 'nice' weddings. In either case he is given pastoral and evangelistic opportunities at a crucial point in peoples' lives. His problem is to seize those opportunities in a way which upholds the ideals of Christian marriage in general, and, in particular, secures the happiness and well-being of the couple being married. A consideration of this dual responsibility is followed by a brief discussion of other problems, mainly of a practical nature, directly related to marriage in church.

1. The ideals of Christian marriage are no longer universally accepted. The pastor, therefore, is in difficulty before any couple ask him to marry them; he faces a sharp conflict between traditional Christian values and modern secular attitudes. If he is to defend Christian teaching against attack, propound it convincingly to others and exercise an effective pastoral ministry among those who seek marriage, his first priority must be to grapple with the

theology of marriage for himself. It is insufficient for him to rely on dogmatic assertion alone — 'this is the church's teaching and must be accepted'. In a society where 'living together' is widely regarded as an acceptable social and economic convenience by no means sinful, he must be able to argue that an intimate personal relationship (however stable and loving) is far richer for being grounded in marriage, marriage which is received as God's gift to man and woman and recognized both as the expression of God's purposes for them and as their commitment to God in each other and to each other in God. In an age when pre-marital and extra-marital sexual encounters raise few eyebrows he must be able to advocate the cause of fidelity in marriage, and plead that only unselfish, complete, sacrificial love (as opposed to selfish lust) between one man and one woman is worthy of God's love for us and a fit instrument of God's creative activity in human life. In face of the tendency among many people to turn to divorce as the first and not the last resort in solving marital problems, he must be prepared to justify the church's teaching that marriage is a lifelong partnership and that God intends set-backs and difficulties in it to be overcome for the mutual enrichment and strengthening of shared life rather than to be used for mutual destruction.

Of course, in wrestling with his theology, the pastor must not forget that, at some time, he will meet a view of marriage that runs directly counter to the present 'liberated' trends; it is a view which claims biblical support for male superiority and dominance in marriage and relegates the woman to a subordinate and dependent status; those who hold it quote their texts and insist on the wife promising to 'obey' in the marriage service. Serious questions are raised by it: what is the true nature of the marriage covenant for the Christian? In what ways are a man and a woman equal or unequal in marriage? What relevance has St Paul's teaching (out of its first century context) for today? In considering these questions and those concerning the differences between the church's teaching and secular attitudes and assumptions, the pastor must aim to equip himself with a clearly reasoned theological understanding of Christian marriage, in both its essential nature and its practical expression. In doing this he lays a firm foundation on which to build an effective pastoral ministry among those who seek marriage in church.

How, then, does the pastor uphold the ideals of Christian marriage, in practice? There may be circumstances when, to do this, he has to consider refusing marriage in church. The laws of his church or his own conscience may not permit him to re-marry divorcees;[3] one of the couple may belong to a non-Christian religion or be a declared atheist and be unable to subscribe to the Christian intention of a church service. In such cases the issues are clear-cut. But what is the pastor to do if he feels that a couple are totally unsuited to each other, or are too immature for the union to have the slightest chance of success, or are rushing into marriage without counting the cost, or even that their sincerity is in doubt? When the issues require the pastor to make a subjective judgment he must think carefully and, if at all possible, consult with colleagues before reaching a decision. It should only be a decision to refuse marriage if he is convinced that the ideals of Christian marriage and his own integrity as a Christian pastor would be betrayed if he acted otherwise. Always, he will realize the importance of being 'open' with the couple concerned and do his utmost to persuade them to withdraw their request, rather than risk having it rejected.

Happily, in the majority of cases, there is no *a priori* reason why Christian marriage should not be granted to couples who seek it. Nevertheless, the pastor's responsibility is to insist on adequate preparation for everyone. Those who have grown up in the church will welcome this, expect it, and already have a sufficient grounding in the Christian faith to make his task comparatively easy. Those who are not church members but who want a church service primarily because it provides the traditional backcloth of Gothic arches, organ and bells for a family occasion, will need to be shown the spiritual significance of the event and its place within the context of the Christian faith. Those who tell him that they wouldn't feel 'properly married' if they weren't married in church, 'in God's sight', need to be told that, wherever they take place, all marriages are 'in God's sight', that marriages in the Register Office are 'binding' contracts and, therefore, 'religious', and that the purpose of a church service is not simply to give religious overtones to a legal agreement! How, then, can the pastor best communicate the distinctive nature of Christian marriage?

Perhaps the most relevant way is to take every couple through the marriage service, step by step, showing how each part expresses an important aspect of Christian teaching. It is useful for the couple themselves to be given a copy of the service so that they can read through the section to be discussed at each session, beforehand. (More than one session will be needed to cover the ground fully.) At the same time, they can be given one of the many helpful marriage preparation books available today[4] and asked to note its contents and argument.

The marriage service itself provides the pastor with an excellent opportunity to advocate the ideals of Christian marriage, not only to the bride and bridegroom but also to their families and friends, many of whom will not have been inside a church since their last family 'occasion'. An address may be part of this advocacy but, if so, it needs to be brief and well 'earthed'; the captive congregation is neither accustomed nor willing to listen to a lengthy theological discourse! In fact, the way the pastor conducts the service achieves more than what he says. If he leads an act of worship which is alive with the Spirit, warm in Christian fellowship, and joyful in its celebration of God's goodness and love, the ideals of Christian marriage become self-evident; those ideals are betrayed if he rushes through the service in an atmosphere of cold and lifeless formality. The pastor should aim to give practical expression to the understanding of the service he expounded in the preparation classes. This enables the wedding couple to express their commitment to each other as an act of Christian love and to experience their marriage as a 'new creation' given and blessed by God to whom it is offered back for the future. It also enables the whole congregation to realize the significance of Christian marriage and encourages the married people present to recall and renew their own marriage vows.

2. The pastor will feel that the couple's future happiness and well-being are best secured if they accept the challenge and live out the ideals of Christian marriage. But he will realize that a Christian understanding of marriage which is limited to matters narrowly termed 'spiritual' is not a firm enough foundation on which to build! *Every* aspect of married life must be seen in a Christian context and couples prepared for the total experience which marriage brings. It is not difficult to list the issues involved: finding somewhere to live, buying a house and building a home; the sexual relationship, birth control and planning a family; earning, sharing, spending and saving money; dealing with in-laws, making friends, living in the community, joining a church; these are some of the more important. The real difficulty

lies in how to help the couple cope with these issues. No pastor is expert in every field, even if he had the time to devote a series of sessions to each couple he prepares for marriage, individually. One solution is for him to deal with the specifically Christian issues himself and, for the rest, to enrol the couple in any course arranged by the local Marriage Guidance Council; this depends on such a course being readily available and has the disadvantage of encouraging a false distinction between 'Christian' and 'secular' topics. A better solution is for local clergy to arrange ecumenical preparation groups (leading up, say, to the Easter or summer weddings); this makes it possible to prepare a larger number of couples together, enables the reticent to feel more at home in the group, and justifies enlisting the help of specialists in the different subjects. A third solution is for the pastor to have a minimum number of sessions with each couple, and then to introduce them to a recently-married husband and wife of similar age and background in his own church, who would invite them to a meal and, we hope, establish a friendship through which experiences could be shared, help given, and problems overcome. All these solutions, however, are counsels of perfection if one of the couple lives in a distant part of the country and is unable to share in preparation classes regularly. If that is the case, the practicalities of the situation must determine the marriage training the pastor gives. However he tackles the problem, he should aim to convince the couple that the many years of married life to which they look forward deserve even more thought and effort in preparation than does their one wedding day; starry-eyed romanticism by itself only leads to happy marriages in fairy tales.

The pastor's responsibility for the couple's happiness and well-being does not end with the last of the preparation classes or with the marriage service; it continues for as long as he and they remain in the same parish. If the couple set up home elsewhere it is important for him to commend them to the pastoral care of a local church and ask that they be warmly welcomed into its worship and fellowship; the possibility of a newly-married couple, who have moved into a new home, forging a new link with the church must not be overlooked. If they set up home locally, a pastoral visit after their return from honeymoon maintains a contact with them; the couple are glad to welcome the pastor as one of their first visitors, to show him the wedding photographs and to recall the various excitements of the wedding day. On such a visit a short prayer of blessing on their new home comes naturally, and they are reminded of the spiritual dimension of their new life together. Having been married in church (whether or not they are church members) they are now part of the church 'family' and within the church's pastoral care. This is a long-term, continuing commitment, of course, although special occasions such as wedding anniversaries, the birth of a child, or a family bereavement give particular opportunities for visits and for ministry. A rededication service for couples married in the church over a period, say, of five years, is sometimes an effective reminder to them that *they* are involved in a Christian commitment, as well as the pastor. But if every effort on his and the church's part fails to win a response from a couple, it is wrong for the pastor to feel a sense of failure and guilt. People's freedom to make their own life outside the Christian community must always be respected and God must be allowed to deal with the situation in his own way. He will!

3. Other problems within the scope of this article concern the practical arrangements for the service, the legal aspects of the pastor's responsibilities, and the question of fees.

People who are not accustomed to attending church or to being in the limelight in any way, are often anxious about being the focus of attention in the unfamiliar setting of a church and having to take a prominent part in a service. The pastor's responsibility, even if he cannot allay their fears entirely, is to put them as much at their ease as possible. One session of the preparation classes needs to be devoted to the 'mechanics' of the Marriage Service, from beginning to end; the couple need to ask their questions: Where do we stand? When do we kneel? Who holds the ring? and so on. The questions may seem trivial to the pastor who has been through the service many times before, but they are very important to people facing a new experience apprehensively. If their questions are answered clearly and fully, and the couple are assured that, when the time comes, nobody in the church will be left in doubt as to what to do, a rehearsal for the service is unnecessary. Indeed, except for state occasions (at St Paul's Cathedral, perhaps!) a rehearsal can prove counter-productive and lead people, on the day itself, to concentrate more on the effort to 'get it right' than on the significance of the service. By maintaining an atmosphere of 'dignified informality' in his conduct of the service, the pastor can deal unobtrusively with any hesitations or mistakes that may occur and ensure that the whole occasion is happy, rather than formidable, for everybody.

Although the legal aspects of marriage only cause problems for the pastor if he acts carelessly or foolishly with regard to them, their importance must never be forgotten. Marriage is not simply a private and personal matter between two individuals; it brings together two previously separate families, it creates a new family unit in the community, and has repercussions for society generally. Marriage, therefore, is properly regulated within the framework of law. There are differences, still, between the legal requirements for a marriage in the established church and for one in a nonconformist church and the pastor should be aware of his own legal position before conducting any marriage service. The nonconformist pastor, for instance, must be satisfied that he is the duly appointed 'authorized person' for the solemnization of marriages (without the presence of the Registrar) and that his church is an officially registered building for that purpose under the Marriage Act. Before a marriage can take place, at the service when declarations of intent are made, and afterwards, when the marriage is registered, there are laws to be kept; any irregularity can invalidate a marriage and cause serious problems and embarrassment for everybody concerned. If difficulties arise (fortunately, a rare occurrence!) clear procedural instructions are contained in the booklet 'Rules and Regulations under the Marriage Act', a copy of which must be kept with the marriage registers in the church safe. But marriage law is not only the concern of the pastor! The marriage couple need both to observe it and to understand its significance. By explaining the legal framework of their marriage to them, the pastor can stress the seriousness of the step they are taking and make clear that marriage is more than a self-centred fulfilment of one person's love for another, it is a contribution to the fabric of human society as a whole and one in the success of which we all have a stake.

Should charges be made for the church's services in marriage? There is no problem here for those churches where statutory fees are paid by everyone, without exception, and the fee received by the pastor is deducted from his salary. Problems only arise where a church exercises discretion in its fees and the pastor has freedom to decide how much to charge or whether to charge at all.

Three factors should be taken into account: couples *expect* to pay for the different services provided by the church at weddings; church fees (at their maximum) only amount to a fraction of the total cost of a family wedding;[5] the organist, the choir, and other busy people expected to officiate at the ceremony deserve a realistic remuneration for their time and services. The pastor is at liberty, however, if he chooses, to forego his own fee. It would seem better, though, for him to charge a standard fee to every couple and, where he is a friend of the family and a guest at the reception, to return it to them in the form of a wedding present. It is unlikely that making a charge will compromise the pastor's ministry in any way; unless it is exorbitant the couple will not hold it against him!

---

[1] In 1970 the total number of marriages in England and Wales was 415,487; in 1979 the comparable figure was 368,853 (Office of Population Censuses and Surveys).

[2] In 1970, of the total, 164,119 were civil marriages; in 1979 these numbered 187,381 (*ibid*).

[3] Problems relating to the re-marriage of divorcees are discussed in the next chapter.

[4] *I give you this ring* by Edward H. Patey (Mowbray [1982], £1·50) is an excellent study course.

[5] At a recent wedding, church fees amounted to £40. The bride's bouquet cost £25. What the champagne cost was not disclosed!

# The Re-marriage of Divorcees in Church

WILLIAM D. HORTON, M.A.
Sevenoaks

WHEN divorcees ask the minister to re-marry them in church, what does he say? Unhappily, there is no commonly agreed *Christian* answer to the question — so much depends on the minister's denomination. If he is a Roman Catholic priest he answers 'no'; his church doesn't recognize divorce and, marriage being indissoluble, there is no such thing as re-marriage. If he is an Anglican incumbent, loyal to his church's discipline, he also answers 'no'; the Church of England, while recognizing divorce and being prepared to give Holy Communion to couples re-married by the secular authority, does not permit their re-marriage in church. If he is a Free Church minister he answers 'maybe'; the main non-conformist denominations recognize divorce and, in certain circumstances, allow re-marriage in church. Of course, not all ministers fit into the prescribed pattern! It is not unknown, for instance, (in real life as well as on 'The Archers'!) for an Anglican priest to sit lightly on canonical obedience and exercise his *legal* right to re-marry divorced people in his church. Nor is it unknown for a Free Church minister, not under the constraints of an imposed discipline, always to refuse requests for re-marriage; there is nothing to compel him to act against his conscience, in any way. Because it is unlikely that a minister worthy of the gospel would marry all-comers simply 'on demand', the basic distinction, therefore, is between those who invariably say 'no' to re-marriage and those who are willing to consider each request on its merits.

Life is much easier for the minister who always says 'no'! For him, the situation is clear-cut and his response to it pre-determined. However fiercely the issue of re-marriage is debated in the councils of the church and whatever his personal sympathies, in his pastoral relationships the minister who exercises a rigid discipline need lose no sleep in deciding what to do. And the rough justice of treating everyone alike may win him a grudging respect from those whose request for re-marriage is refused. It may even win him a degree of understanding of his position if he lays the blame for his refusal at the door of a higher author- ity — 'However much I'd like to be able to help, I'm sorry I can't, *the church* won't allow it'.

The situation is very different for the minister whose church gives *him* the responsibility of deciding whether or not to re-marry divorcees. First, of course, he needs to wrestle with the question of principle; is it right for him to re-marry, in church, anyone who has been married before and whose previous partner is still living? If he is prepared to admit the general principle how, then, does he come to a decision in particular cases? For him, the situation is never clear-cut because no two requests are alike and the factors influencing his response are always different. There may be suggested guide-lines to help him reach a decision; he may have colleagues and superiors to whom he can (while respecting confidentiality) turn for consultation and advice. In the end, however, he himself carries the heavy burden of responsibility for saying 'yes' or 'no'. When the buck stops with him how can the local minister decide what action to take? And when he's made a decision (whatever it is) how does he maintain and strengthen a pastoral relationship with the people most affected by it? The two problems of general principle and practical application are the main concern of this article; the third problem, that of pastoral care, is the subject of a brief concluding paragraph. It is foolish to imagine that there is a simple solution to any of them or that they can be dealt with by a set of fixed rules; it is important to consider the issues involved in the hope that the way through the minefield may be seen more clearly!

## General Principles

The minister's decision about whether or not to re-marry divorcees at all isn't left to the moment when the first couple to ask him for re-marriage stand on his doorstep! If he has had good pastoral training, he will have faced the general question of re-marriage and come to certain conclusions before meeting the real-life situation. If he seeks to keep abreast of the contemporary discussion about the principles involved he need not lack help as much of value has been written, recently, on the subject. Space permits mention of only two documents, *Marriage, Divorce and the Church*[1] and the counterblast to it *For Better For Worse*.[2] Although written from an Anglican standpoint, reflecting opposing arguments within the Church of England, both highlight the issues facing ministers of all denominations in a thought-provoking and informative manner. But when all the books have been read and all the arguments carefully weighed up, what are the determinative questions to which answers must be given before a judgment is made, in principle? The four which follow are among the more important and are closely inter-related.

1. What is the teaching of scripture? It is easier to list the relevant passages than to interpret them! Central to the question is the teaching of Jesus. There is little doubt that our Lord stressed the pivotal importance of marriage in human relationships and believed it God's intention that the 'one flesh' he creates should be a permanent union. There is

little doubt, also, that Christ's saying forbidding divorce was more accurately reported by Mark and Luke than by Matthew[3] who allowed the exception of adultery. On these grounds, some argue that as Jesus regarded marriage as indissoluble and re-marriage as sinful, so he laid down an inflexible rule for his followers everywhere, for all time. Others argue, however, that Jesus was only concerned with the specific, Jewish, situation of his own day. Jewish law gave men dominance in marital affairs while women were treated as property to be used (and divorced) at will. Of course Jesus prohibited divorce when, every time, the woman was the loser! Our present situation is very different, and Christ's response to his contemporary problem ought not to be codified into universal and permanent law. In any case (the argument continues) Jesus always advocated love, not law, as the foundation of human behaviour; we must seek to interpret the spirit of his teaching and not be bound by its letter. Christ's ideal of life-long marriage must not become a mill-stone for all who fall short of it. The minister seeking to make up his mind about re-marriage on the basis of scripture is faced, therefore, with two alternatives. He must give greater weight to one or the other.

2. How is the gospel best proclaimed? The church's responsibility to preach the gospel isn't discharged when Sunday's sermons have been delivered! It is essential for the good news of God's love in Christ to be embodied in every part of the church's life and work. What the church *does* must be as much 'gospel' as what it *says* (especially as, for many people today, what the church does *is* what it says). How then does the minister preach the gospel in the context of the re-marriage of divorcees? Does he do it by allowing re-marriage — as a testimony to God's forgiveness of sin, God's power to 'make all things new' (Rev 21[5]) and God's love which wills satisfying fulfilment for his children in

their marital relationships? Or does he do it by refusing re-marriage on the grounds that he thereby witnesses to the constancy of love (*agape* rather than *eros*) as the only true foundation of human happiness, and to the grace of God which can bring good out of evil when it is suffered for righteousness' sake? Both positions are open to attack: the former as sub-Christian sentimentalism which betrays the gospel and the latter as harsh legalism which denies it. The minister must decide which proclaims the gospel better.

3. How should the church respond to secular pressures? The rapid changes, over recent years, in society's attitude to marriage, divorce and related issues, give a particular reference to this general question. The present divorce laws, the willingness of the state to re-marry divorcees and the large number who seek re-marriage, the feeling of many ordinary people that much of what our Christian fore-fathers believed about marital, pre-marital and extra-marital relationships was hypocritical, or misguided, or harmful (or all three!) — these things bring pressure on the church to re-examine its attitudes and practices. How should the church react to the pressure? Some answer that in times of (what they term) moral laxity the church must stand firm as the bastion of traditional, proven, values; they are not prepared to countenance re-marriage in church. Others answer that God speaks not only to the world through the church but, equally, through the world to the church; movements in modern secular thought and behaviour may be of God rather than the devil. Those who accept this premise and are willing to question whether long-established Christian principles are as Christian or as unchangeable as it is claimed, may also be willing to consider re-marriage in church.

4. How is the ideal of Christian marriage best upheld? The Christian ideal of marriage has always been that of a

life-long union of one man and one woman. Of course, that
ideal is best upheld by couples who, until parted by death,
fulfil God's purposes for their lives and so experience his
blessing in this most sacred, intimate and loving of all
human relationships. In a perfectly Christian world no
doubt all marriages would attain that ideal! In the real
world not all do. Many marriages, though never terminated
in the courts, fall very far short of perfection; one in three
marriages contracted today ends in divorce. Christians are
divided as to how best to uphold their ideals in this situation
and three different approaches were noted at the beginning
of this article. Those who regard a marriage as eternally
indissoluble argue that vows which are solemnly made
before God and which commit two people to each other on
the deepest level of their beings, for life, are of such a
binding and sacramental character that divorce and, therefore, re-marriage are out of the question. The critics of this
(so called) 'high' view of marriage claim that, in practice, it
does the church a disservice. By refusing to admit that
marriages *are* broken and that love *does* die, it takes no
account of human sin and frailty and imprisons many
couples in an empty form of union from which all Christian
content has gone. Those who allow divorce but not re-marriage tread the way of compromise! They recognize that
marriages fail but hold that Christian marriage is brought
into disrepute and marriage vows devalued by permitting
divorcees a 'second chance' to form a successful union with
the church's blessing. The critics of this second approach
argue that its harshness in condemning a Christian divorcee
to loneliness or to a secular marriage fails in Christian
compassion. Those who allow both divorce and re-marriage in church are attacked by the proponents of the other
two approaches for 'conceding the corner' they are fighting
hard to hold. To permit re-marriage may indeed carry the

risk of abuse, but, in favour, it must be said that many divorcees, older and wiser as a result of their previous experience, bring to their second marriage a depth of commitment and a maturity which are often lacking in a first marriage and which express rather than deny the Christian ideal. On this question, too, the minister who has freedom to do so must take his stand on what he believes to be the firmest ground.

## Practical Application

If, after much thought, a minister accepts the principle of marrying divorcees in church, how does he decide what to do in practice? What factors are determinative in leading him to say either 'yes' or 'no' to any particular request for re-marriage? Obviously, the decision he takes must reflect and not deny the premises on which he based his 'in principle' judgment. It must, for instance, proclaim the gospel in the given situation and not flout Christian standards. But that is not as easy as it sounds! No situation involving personal relationships is ever clear-cut and no two such situations are exactly alike. Only after spending time and care in getting to know each couple, learning about the circumstances of their particular request and weighing the arguments for and against their re-marriage will he be able to make a decision and feel persuaded of its basic 'rightness'.

An interview with the couple, therefore, is essential. Because of its importance it needs to be by appointment for a time when the minister isn't under the constraint of his next engagement. And, if its purpose is to be achieved, it needs to be in the right setting and carefully prepared. Neither the minister nor the couple is helped by a fifteen-minute interrogation in a cheerless vestry! When faced with an inquisition of that nature, people who (through fear of rebuff) are diffident about approaching the minister at all are put on the defensive, made to feel under the church's condemnation for their past failures and placed at a disadvantage in expressing themselves adequately. The wise minister interviews people in the relaxed and friendly atmosphere of a comfortable lounge (over coffee?) and seeks to achieve his ends by first gaining their confidence. He then obtains the information he needs to form a judgment not by asking a long list of questions but by skilfully leading the conversation to reveal points he feels are significant. The three which follow ought to be included among them:

1. *Motives.* Why do the couple seek a church rather than a Register Office wedding? Because, as practising Christians,[4] they want their marriage solemnized in a Christian context? Or because, although not church-goers, they 'believe in God' and feel they wouldn't be 'properly married' without a church service? Or is it because the prospective bride (or her mother!) wants a traditional, wedding against a church backcloth? It is worthwhile probing motives; the couple expect to be asked and come prepared with their answer. If the minister uncovers the reasons for their request (the real reasons, not necessarily those advanced at first!) he is in a position to evaluate the situation more accurately, to determine what the Christian response ought to be to it, and to see how the conversation can be brought round to the significance of Christian marriage.

2. *The significance of Christian marriage.* Here the minister's first responsibility is not to lecture the couple on *his* view of Christian marriage but to elicit from them *their* understanding of it. What, for instance, is the real difference between a church and a Register Office wedding?

He ought not to be surprised if little is revealed! Nor ought he to refuse re-marriage on that ground alone. After all, many 'first-timers' are woefully deficient in Christian understanding and he doesn't necessarily reject *them*. The couple's hesitant and inadequate comments must be built on to highlight the sacredness of vows, the religious nature of the marriage bond, the meaning of the symbolism used in the Marriage Service, its prayers and its spiritual content so that, at the end of the conversation, he knows whether or not they are 'open' to Christian ideas, willing to accept the implications of a service in church, and ready to take these matters further in marriage preparation classes.

3. *Self-awareness*. The two previous points ought to be discussed with every couple seeking a church marriage. So, of course, ought the third although, where divorcees and their proposed new partners are concerned, self-awareness is particularly relevant. Only after motives and meanings have been discussed (not before) can the past be introduced into the conversation in any creative way. In the light of what has been said about Christian marriage how does the divorcee see himself/herself in relation to the first union and its break-up? What has been learned from that experience which will provide a firmer basis for a new marriage? The words 'sin' and 'repentance' may not be used, but the minister will look for evidence of realism, a measure of self-criticism and an acknowledgement of failure. If he only finds that the other partner is blamed, the divorce is glossed over as 'just one of those things' and there is blind optimism that, of course, all will be well next time, he will hesitate to countenance re-marriage in church.

## Pastoral Care

When (humanly speaking) everything has been considered and time allowed for reflection, however difficult it may be for him, the minister has to make a decision. Whether favourable or unfavourable, the file isn't closed when the couple have been informed of it! There are important pastoral responsibilities still to fulfil. If he agrees to a re-marriage there are opportunities for pre-wedding counselling, for celebrating the gospel at the wedding itself and, afterwards, for incorporating the newly-married couple into the life of the worshipping community. If he refuses re-marriage then there are problems. These aren't solved by offering a church 'service of blessing' after the Register Office ceremony. It seems hypocritical to ask God's blessing on a union that the church isn't prepared to solemnize in his name! The couple, feeling rejected themselves, are almost bound to reject the church and there is little the minister can do, as the focus of that rejection, to heal the wounds. Only loving Christian neighbours and friends have any hope of eventually effecting a reconciliation. The minister must pray that this may be achieved — as he must also pray that, in reaching his decision, he did not altogether betray the heart and mind of Christ.

---

[1] The Report of the Commission on the Christian Doctrine of Marriage (SPCK, Fifth impression [1975]).

[2] A Symposium on Marriage edited by Cheslyn Jones (the Church Union, Second edition [1977]).

[3] Mt 19[9], 5[32], Mk 10[11], Lk 16[18].

[4] What if the couple are loyal members of another church? Until there is a commonly accepted marriage discipline no minister need feel bound to uphold another denomination's rules. He must act according to his own church discipline and his own conscience. Significantly, many ministers who are unable to act in the matter themselves recommend divorcees to ministers who can.

# Funerals

WILLIAM D. HORTON, M.A.
Sevenoaks

FUNERALS, like the poor, are always with us. The universality of death and of the 'religious' streak in human nature ensure that. However successfully people may suppress their spiritual self when life goes smoothly, that self comes to the surface in times of crisis. By no means all children born, today, into a traditionally Christian society are baptized; not every marriage takes place in church; but it is still a very rare occurrence for a person's mortal remains to be disposed of without some form of religious observance. The pastor, therefore, is brought into close, personal contact with many families apart from those of his own church membership and is given the opportunity of ministering to people who would not otherwise call on him for help. But the opportunity brings its problems: How is the gospel to be preached effectively in the context of death and bereavement? How can the love of Christ be ministered to people in their grief? How can the dead be remembered in a worthy manner? This article is concerned, primarily, with the first two of these problems; the third is discussed, briefly, in section 3; section 4 deals, equally briefly, with related matters which can also cause difficulty. Discussion must not be restricted to the funeral itself but must include the days leading up to, and the months following, the service. It must not be restricted, either, to bereavement in families with no obvious Christian commitment or church affiliation; even when a life-long Christian dies peacefully at home, strengthened by Christian hope and surrounded by the love of a Christian family, problems arise. *Every* funeral brings its challenges and the pastor must be prepared to meet them.

## 1. *Preaching the gospel*

In the nature of the case, people are most receptive to the gospel at times of need; good news means more to them at funerals than at weddings! Aware of their inadequacy in face of death and of the darkness of their grief they are ready to hear the word of God. The pastor, therefore, starts with an advantage and, where the mourners are loyal members of the Christian family, he seizes the opportunity of building on their Christian experience and of reminding them of their faith in the living Christ and his promises of eternal life. But what is he to do when his hearers don't know Christ, when they have only a nodding acquaintance with the church and, in all probability, only a distorted understanding of the Christian message? And what is he to preach when the deceased never darkened the doors of a church during his lifetime and, apparently, displayed few of the graces of Christian living?

In every case he preaches the same gospel in the same way! He preaches Christ! He speaks of God's love for the world revealed in 'the man for others'; of the compassionate ministry Jesus exercised among the sorrowful, lonely and despairing of his own day; of the defeat of death through Christ's cross and resurrection; of the living Saviour's presence with all who turn to him in their need, today. He offers God's forgiveness in Christ to all who will accept it and, then, he leaves it at that!

By making his preaching Christ-centred the pastor avoids two pitfalls which face him. First, he avoids making judgments. Whether he believes that, in the end, all men will be saved, or that only those who commit their lives to

Christ now will live with him hereafter, his theological stance must never lead him into a judgmental attitude. Whether or not he believes in the reality of a hell after death, as well as of a heaven, his belief must never betray him into frightening, cajoling or threatening those whom grief makes especially vulnerable. In the final analysis, no pastor, however perceptive, can gauge a fellow human being's standing with God. He cannot possibly know what is in the heart of the worst so-called 'sinner'; nor can he know the secret weaknesses and failures of the so-called 'saint'. Only God knows what is in a man and God's prerogative of judgment must not be usurped. The pastor's task is to preach Christ, in whose light all (without exception) have sinned and come under judgment; to preach Christ, in whom God offers forgiveness to all men and a judgment in love and mercy. If he cannot, in all conscience, speak *good* news at every funeral, let him keep quiet at them all!

Second, through Christ-centred preaching the pastor avoids giving credence to some of the sub-Christian attitudes to death popularly held today. It is a misrepresentation of the gospel to pretend, as some do, that death is an illusion and that man, by nature, is immortal; the clear witness of scripture is 'Christ died'. To minimize the significance of death in the hope of bringing comfort to the bereaved is to offer little consolation to those who are acutely aware of its reality. The opposite belief, that death brings extinction and oblivion, has a wider currency; by preaching Christ who 'rose from the dead on the third day' the pastor proclaims the Christian assurance of life beyond the grave and offers the Christian hope of heaven. There are occasions, too, when the pastor must strongly deny the truth of a frequently held notion that every death is according to God's purposes. 'The Lord gave and the Lord hath taken away' is an OT and not a Christian text! The family of a young mother who died from cancer, the friends of a teenager tragically killed in a motor-cycle accident, relatives of people who lost their lives in a natural disaster, must not be encouraged in the blasphemy that everything which happens in life is 'God's will'. By preaching Christ who, himself, faced our world of evil, tragedy and free-will and who died, violently, while fighting against everything that thwarts God's loving purposes for mankind, the pastor can confidently declare that God is never unaware of human suffering, nor unmoved by human grief. God stands with all who are victims of cruel circumstances ready (as he was, in Christ) to transform their evil into good, their death into resurrection life. There are no quick or simple answers in the face of questioning grief and the pastor must not imagine he can provide them. He can only point people to Christ, and unless his words speak of that Word they are spoken in vain.

## 2. *Ministering to the bereaved*

The pastor's ministry to the bereaved begins as soon as he hears of the death; it is important to visit the family at the earliest opportunity. From the outset, two things need to be remembered: first, bereavement is invariably an emotional shock and, second, emotions other than grief are often present and must be recognized.

However much a death is expected (and even welcomed, where great suffering has been involved), however calmly the sorrow is borne, there is always a traumatic element in facing the death of a loved one or friend; life cannot proceed unruffled. Many people are quite unprepared to meet the shock of bereavement. Today, when a long expectation of life is normal and early death, through disease, is no longer a grim spectre haunting every family, when the dying are taken from home into hospital and 'death' has replaced 'sex' as the taboo subject of conversation, people don't live with death as previous generations did. When death comes, therefore, they need help in facing up to it and the pastor's responsibility is to respond to that need. Words of sympathy, of course, are appropriate, but a warm handshake can express as much, if not more, than the most carefully chosen words. Undue piety, sepulchral gloom and, certainly, false cheerfulness must be avoided at all costs. Again, it is better to say nothing than to urge the mourners to pull themselves together and smile! In a situation where neighbours and friends may feel 'awkward' and reluctant to intrude on what they consider to be private grief, the pastor gives greatest help by being present, by being his natural self, and so assuring the family that they are not alone. There may be practical help he can give: 'phoning the undertaker, informing relatives, explaining procedures, making tea. In his supportive role he enables the family to accept the reality and face the shock of bereavement.

The pastor's responsibility is also to recognize that emotions other than grief may be present in the situation. He can only minister effectively when he is aware of these emotions. There may be remorse and a sense of guilt that more wasn't done for the deceased; bitterness at the unfairness of death; self-pity; a feeling of being let down when fervent prayers don't seem to have been answered; worry about what happens after death; fear of a lonely future. None of these emotions, necessarily, will be self-evident; people are adept at hiding their true feelings from others. The pastor's task is to be the catalyst for bringing them out into the open, in the knowledge that healing, comfort and peace of mind are only possible as the truth is honestly faced. He must, therefore, be a good listener; he must encourage the bereaved to 'let go' before he can offer the ministry of Christ in love and friendship. That ministry will vary with the particular needs of the people but, invariably, will include the ministry of prayer. The pastor's offer to pray with the family is not likely to be refused; it is usually welcomed and appreciated. By giving thanks for their loved one's life, by bringing their need before God and asking for his strength to meet it, the pastor exercises an invaluable ministry of comfort and care.

The funeral itself provides an opportunity for ministry which ought not to be taken for granted. The pastor needs to discuss details of the service, beforehand, with the relatives so that they are made aware of its form. If he invites their requests for the service, he mustn't be surprised if they ask for the traditional hymns and readings. He may feel that 'Abide with me' is somewhat threadbare through over-use, but people who have only a tenuous hold on the faith find greater help and comfort in the familiar rites of folk-religion than they do in unfamiliar expressions of worship, however preferable to him. He also needs to ensure that the church is warm and welcoming, the organist and sidesmen are on duty and flowers are arranged (funerealism helps nobody!).

The service must be one of Christian worship. At this point, the most effective ministry the pastor can offer people is to turn their thoughts, away from themselves and their own need, to God, living, eternal, merciful and loving. In meeting God's love in Christ, life and death are seen in true perspective and mourners find strength for that day and hope for the future. In conducting the service, the pastor's main problem is to strike the right balance between a cold formalism and an over-emotional approach. To rush through a service with scarcely a mention of the deceased's name offers little comfort to anybody; to make it too lengthy and too personal is to place the mourners, who have had to steel themselves to face the occasion, under an unfair pressure when they are least able to bear it. Professionalism (in the true sense) demands that the pastor leads the service with reverence, dignity and an objectivity which allows him to 'personalize' the occasion in the way he feels best.

The most distressing moment of the funeral, for the mourners, is when the coffin is lowered into the grave (is it *really* necessary for earth to be scattered on the coffin?) or the curtains are drawn round the catafalque in the crematorium. This moment should not be prolonged especially if, at a burial, the weather is bad. The pastor has exercised an effective ministry in the service if, when the physical body of the deceased disappears from view, the mourners are content to leave their loved one with God, in childlike trust.

It is when the service is over that the pastor's ministry to the bereaved becomes vitally important! He is often expected to go back to the house, afterwards. He may feel it right to accept the invitation, but with relatives and friends sharing memories and conversation he has no particular part to play. However, when family and friends are gone and the world resumes its normal business, his ministry (and that of the local church) comes into its own. People who are buoyed up doing all those necessary jobs which so usefully occupy time and attention before a funeral find that, afterwards, there is time to spare and the sadness of their loss weighs more heavily on them; those who haven't immediate or nearby family are especially vulnerable to loneliness. Frequent visiting of such folk, both by the pastor and by church members, is essential; church flowers must be sent, anniversaries remembered and the church's fellowship expressed in every way possible. This is a long-term responsibility; on being faithful to it, the pastor helps the bereaved person readjust to life and find, in the caring of others, an experience of Christ himself.

### 3. *Remembering the dead*

A funeral service is a memorial service and the congregation expects it to be a worthy tribute to the deceased. The pastor has little difficulty in speaking of someone he knew well as a loyal church member. His problem, in this case, is to avoid overstating his case in a fulsome eulogy; the entirely sanctified are few and far between! A short tribute, free of sentimentality, highlighting the life and character of the deceased and giving thanks to God for him (warts and all!) is most appropriate. The difficulty is greater when the pastor never met the deceased and the first contact he has with the family is when he is asked to conduct the funeral. How can he pay any tribute in these circumstances? He is greatly helped by the readiness of bereaved people to talk about their loved one; in his visits prior to the funeral he can glean much useful information and, without in any way interrogating the family and friends, can discover what he wishes to know (a piece of card on which to jot down the salient facts as soon as he's left the house, is an aid to memory later!). By building up a mental picture of the deceased, in this way, he is able to pay a tribute both true and sincere, at the service.

A tribute doesn't need to be in the form of an address. Prayers can also be used as a vehicle of remembrance and many pastors prefer to give thanks for a person's life through them rather than through an address. If so, let them be short prayers, thanking God for happy memories; let them be direct prayers, highlighting the various facets of the person's life and work; and let them include brief periods of silence in which members of the congregation can, individually, remember the deceased and offer personal thanksgiving to God.

## 4. *Related problems*

These concern cooperation with the undertaker and fees. The majority of undertakers provide a courteous, helpful and efficient service to the bereaved; the success of their business depends on satisfied customers! In the majority of cases, too, the relationship between the pastor and the undertaker is good; each needs the other in his work and friendly cooperation between them is essential. Occasionally, however, difficulties arise. It is not unknown, for example, for an undertaker to arrange the date and time of a funeral without consulting the pastor and then to expect him to officiate whatever other engagements he may have had for that day. In spite of the undertaker's need to book times at the cemetery or (more urgently) at the crematorium, and to fit in with the convenience of the family, there are few occasions when this discourtesy is excusable. If it is a frequent occurrence the pastor is justified in reminding the undertaker that his diary also needs to be consulted and that there may be occasions when *his* schedule must determine the day and the time of a funeral. It is usually sufficient for the point to be made for better cooperation to follow.

Some pastors are also concerned with the high cost of dying today, and the inadequacy of the death grant to meet more than a fraction of the undertaker's bill. They know that elderly people in their churches are often worried that their slender resources won't meet the expenses of their funeral and it is a matter of pride for them that they are not indebted to anyone when death comes. It must be realized, however, that undertaking is labour-intensive and costs are bound to be high. If there is evidence of excessive charges by a particular undertaker, the matter should be discussed in the clergy fraternal or Council of Churches and some common action agreed. But experience suggests that many undertakers adjust their charges according to the customer's ability to pay and, by the rich helping the poor, rough justice is achieved. Also, in addition to his normal service, the undertaker can be asked to provide a more basic service at lower cost. It is, perhaps, regrettable that the pastor receives a funeral fee which, often, is regarded as part of his income. If the pastor feels that his ministry to the bereaved is compromised by receiving a fee from them (albeit indirectly) he may either decline to accept it from the undertaker or accept it and return it, privately, to the family. The former alternative offers no certainty that the deduction will be passed on in any composite bill to the family; the latter can be the source of personal embarrassment. In facing this dilemma, the individual pastor must act as he feels best in the particular situation. Problems, too, like the poor, are always with us!

# Part III
# The Pastor's Caring

# Visiting

WILLIAM D. HORTON, M.A.
Sevenoaks

Wide was his parish, with houses far asunder,
Yet he neglected not in rain or thunder,
In sickness, or in trouble, to pay call
On the remotest whether great or small
Upon his feet, and in his hand a stave. . . .

Chaucer: *The Prologue to Canterbury Tales*

'Is he a good visitor?' Invariably, that question is asked whenever a church seeks a new minister.[1] The conviction is widespread that, in building up the church, faithful pastoral care expressed in home visiting[2] is even more important than good preaching, sound teaching and efficient administration. Chaucer speaks for Christians living in very different times and situations from our own when he gives the stamp of approval to his 'poor parson', a diligent and devoted under-shepherd of the Good Shepherd himself. Not for him jaunts to the city to court favours of the fashionable and wealthy —

He stayed at home and watched over his fold
So that no wolf should make the sheep miscarry.
He was a shepherd and no mercenary.

'Amen to that', says the congregation, today!

For various reasons, today's pastor cannot share the congregation's conviction so fervently. He is not always convinced that the traditional pattern of visiting is the only way, or even the best way, of exercising a pastoral role. A ministry well suited to the pastoral and mainly static society of previous centuries may be out of place in the urbanized, very mobile society in which most people live today; a changed world demands changed methods of caring. Even if he does regard visiting as important, he cannot be unaware of the problems involved. The purpose of this article is to identify those problems, to suggest practical ways of overcoming them, and then to indicate how the opportunities afforded by pastoral visiting can best be used. This will be done in the two contexts of the church community and the wider community beyond. But it is a worthwhile exercise only if there are compelling reasons why visiting should still have a high place on the pastor's list of priorities. The question of motives, therefore, must be discussed first.

*Why visit at all?*

Any pastor who finds visiting uncongenial, or too demanding, or who wants an excuse for *not* doing it, need not look far for arguments to support him. He may say that visiting is simply a hang-over from Victorian and Edwardian days when the socially conscious had their 'at homes' and 'returned visits' and 'left cards', and that it has no more place in today's ministry than in society generally. Similarly, he may say that the time has passed (if, indeed, it were ever present!) when home visiting was necessary to ensure a church-going people. He knows only too well that if the motive for visiting is to fill the pews, by encouraging the faithful and reminding the absentees of their responsibilities, it is both unworthy and ineffective. Or, he may feel that, in visiting, all he is really doing is helping to prop up the institutional church by seeking support for this or that project, collecting money for one fund or another, and the interests of God's kingdom are better served in other ways. And they probably are if that's the purpose of visiting!

No! A practice commended in the NT (see Mt 25[36], Jas 1[27]) and observed so widely in the church, from the beginning until now, obviously stems from something more than social custom or the desire to ensure the successful continuance of the institution. It has its root in theology! As, through the incarnate Christ, God gave flesh and bones to his love for the world and took the initiative in meeting people on their own ground, so the pastor goes out in Christ's name, today, representing his Body, the church, for no other motive than that of mediating the grace of God to people, whoever they are and whatever their situation. Through visiting, he establishes relationships with individuals and with families in a way not possible through a few moments' conversation after a service or meeting. He comes to know people on their own ground where they are most truly themselves — at home. He becomes aware of their gifts and graces, their hopes and fears, their needs and the problems they face, and is able to bring to bear on all of them a spiritual dimension. He offers himself as the instrument through which God can work in people's lives, today. Whatever reasons others may have for visiting, the reason the pastor visits is to give practical expression to God's love and care for all the members of his family. And that is a compelling enough reason for the pastor to take seriously the problems facing him and to do his best to solve them.

## Visiting in the church community

Today's pastor faces two problems, at least, which were unfamiliar to his predecessors of not many years ago: finding a suitable time to visit and making clear to his church members the purpose of a pastoral call. From the pastor's point of view the ideal time to visit is the afternoon; many older ministers were trained to be in their studies in the morning, in people's homes in the afternoon, and at meetings in the evening. However helpful that simple

division of time may still be to the pastor, it has little
relevance to most church situations today. People are not
often found at home in the afternoon; wives as well as
husbands go to work, mothers take their children out,
senior citizens join in the multifarious activities provided
for their interest and only the permanently house-bound are
certain to be in. Nothing is more disheartening (and
wasteful of petrol) than an afternoon spent in abortive
visiting! Evening visits may be possible for the pastor whose
schedule of meetings allows them, and families are more
likely to be at home then. But with everybody watching
television in the only living room, any interruption of their
favourite programme is always bound to be resented by
some members of the family. That leaves the morning!
Pre-occupation with necessary domestic chores leaves most
people unprepared for visitors then, unless they call by
prior arrangement.

How can this problem be solved? Some would say it can
only be solved by following the doctor's example — calling
on those who ask for a home visit and, for the rest,
arranging a 'vestry hour' when any needing help can come
to the minister. But this destroys the idea of the pastor
'going out' in Christ's name and deprives him of the great
advantages of a home contact with all but a few of his
members. Others would solve the problem by announcing,
in advance, what areas they hope to visit on certain days.
Apart from the fact that, unavoidably, such plans have
sometimes to be altered, this method has the disadvantage
of encouraging formality and preparedness (the best china
ready, on a tray!) among those who look forward to a visit
and of giving those who don't the opportunity of being out!
Surely, the best way of facing the difficulty is by applying a
mixture of common sense, careful enquiry and trial-and-
error. If the pastor is flexible enough in the arrangement of

his own programme he will be able to discover those times when a family is glad to see visitors and is receptive to the church's initiative. But however carefully visits are planned, there are bound to be occasions when the pastor calls at an inconvenient time. It is better, then, to retreat gracefully than to stand one's ground. At least, there is the opportunity to ask when it would be convenient to call. There are bound to be occasions, also, when the family is out. To leave a note scribbled on a visiting card or the back of an envelope ('sorry to find you out' is not the happiest phraseology, though!) encourages the family to respond to the visit by suggesting a time when they would be in and happy to see the pastor. In cases of particular difficulty the wise pastor will invite people to *his* home for coffee and a chat — a relationship established in this way develops further when the pastor's invitation is reciprocated later.

The second problem of making clear to people the purpose of a pastoral visit is equally difficult. Everyone knows why the doctor, the social worker and the insurance agent call. But what does the pastor call for? Gone are the days when the pastor visited (and people knew he visited) to catechize the children, to enquire after the spiritual life of the older members of the family and, in cases of need, to take gifts from his larder. Gone, too, are the days when he was greeted with reverence because of his 'cloth' and his visit was an 'occasion' because of what it involved. Generally, church members are pleased to have a visit from the pastor (so long as it's not 'Wimbledon fortnight' or 'Cup Final' day!).

But they are unaware, for the most part, that there may be more to it than a friendly social call or a solicitous enquiry at a time of illness. Not many families, today, have corporate prayer or Bible reading or spiritual conversation on which the pastor can build; any attempt to take the visit beyond mundane pleasantries is difficult and may be resisted. How, in this situation, can the pastor achieve something for the kingdom of God? How can he give the lie to the jibe that visiting is 'drinking tea with old ladies' and not really a job of work at all?

The solution of the problem lies, largely, within the pastor's own hands. If he carefully adopts a professional approach to all his visiting, in the end, the message gets through: people realize that he calls not simply as a friend or social worker but as a man of God. In this context, 'professionalism' involves the pastor in visiting *all* his members and not just those whom he finds congenial or who boost his ego ('How good of you to call when you're so busy'!). It means spending what time is necessary on each call, neither rushing on to the next home, nor outstaying his welcome. It means giving his undivided attention to the people he's with at the moment and making evident his care for them all. It means being open to the Holy Spirit's guidance and sensitive to people's needs, in what he says and how he handles the visit. Because of his professional attitude to his pastoral responsibilities, people will come to see that he is not a hireling but a representative of Christ, the Good Shepherd, and that, whenever he enters a home, he has a distinctive work to do.

Given that the family is at home and that there is some understanding of what a pastoral call signifies how, then, can the opportunities of the visit be best used? If it is part of the pastor's professionalism to be open to the guidance of the Holy Spirit no hard and fast rules can be given. Every visit is bound to be different because every person visited is different. Several points of general import can, however, be made. For instance, every visit should provide an opportunity for the visited person to talk and for the visitor to listen. Pastors who are used to speaking and are facile (in the best sense) in the use of words can sometimes destroy the effectiveness of a visit by completely monopolizing a conversation, in the belief that their task is to talk, to advise and to provide the answers. But more people are helped by having somebody to talk to than having somebody to talk to them! The importance of careful listening cannot be stressed too much. The skilful pastor will know how and when to phrase the leading question that encourages even the most retiring person to 'open up' and brings the conversation round to matters of the spirit. He will also know, from listening to people, how to recognize 'danger signs' and cries for help. The latter may not be spoken aloud, but they can be *sensed* and the pastor should be on the alert for them. Some of the problems may be beyond his ability, as a general practitioner, to deal with effectively, and this he should acknowledge. But to be aware of them is important. With the family's permission, they can be referred to a specialist and, we hope, solved.

Apart from a willingness to listen and to share in conversation, there are other things the pastor has to offer in his visiting. It may not be necessary or theologically justifiable to take Holy Communion to people who share in the sacrament in church, with the whole family of local believers. It may be, however, that Holy Communion could be offered much more frequently to the elderly, the sick and the house-bound than seems to be the practice (I speak, primarily, of the Free Churches). Prayer, too, is another means of grace which ought not to be overlooked. Not that the pastor will pray with the family on every visit! There are occasions when prayer flows naturally from conversation; there is no difficulty in praying when the family has suffered bereavement, or is going through a crisis time, or there is a special event like a wedding or a house-warming. But there are occasions when to pray openly would be unwelcome or would appear to be 'forced'; if prayer is offered because it is the 'done thing' it is hard to justify. Whatever happens *in* the home, however, the true pastor asks God's blessing on the call before he knocks on the door and, after the visit, commits the family and its needs to him. Every visit should thus be made in the context of prayer. Although the pastor's role is different from that of the social worker, there may be times when his part is to offer practical help, particularly where elderly people live on their own are concerned. If there are opportunities of proclaiming the pastoral care of the church in deed as well as word, they should not be missed.

The people most likely to need such practical help are also those most likely to appreciate it if the pastor has 'a cup of tea' with them. He may do much good, in these cases, if he accepts hospitality. He may feel that, in other homes too, a cup of tea enables a conversation to develop in a way it wouldn't do without it and that, therefore, it is worthwhile. But let him beware of giving offence by accepting hospitality from some families and refusing it from others! And let him remember that there is no such thing as 'quick-brew tea'! Unless the tea is already made when he calls or he considers the time waiting for the kettle to boil justified, it is perhaps better to concentrate on more important things.

*Visiting in the wider community*

Much of the foregoing applies as much to visiting in the community as it does to visiting within the church fellowship. But other problems and opportunities, too, are present in neighbourhood visitation. Presuming that the pastor is aware of his responsibilities towards the community generally (Jn 10[16]) and is prepared to leave the security of the church environment for the rougher world outside, what are the particular problems here? Space only permits the mention of two.

First, there is the problem of numbers. The sheer size of the non-church-going community is as difficult for the conscientious pastor of the 'gathered' church to cope with as it is for the Anglican incumbent with his geographical parish. The temptation is to sit back and do nothing! But a useful beginning can be made by visiting (more than once?) those families who still turn to the church for baptism, weddings and funerals. Christian insights can be related to the family's joys and sorrows and a caring relationship established. Visits can also be made to people introduced to the pastor by members of his congregation or met by him outside the life of the church. These are valuable contacts and should be built upon for Christ's sake. But such visiting should not be left to the pastor working on his own! His members must recognize their responsibilities as fellow workers with him in the mission of the whole church and accept an active role in caring for people in their own area, being ready to welcome new residents and visiting their neighbours in the name of the church. If all this can be done ecumenically the problem is shared and more likely to be solved effectively.

The second problem concerns the 'content' of the visit. How does the pastor use his opportunity to the full? Of course, by being himself, by being 'professional' and by being open to the Holy Spirit (these are in no way contradictory!). His task is not to thrust religion upon people, nor to make them feel guilty about their non-attendance at church. Rather, it is to make clear where he stands and to open up channels of communication between different interpretations of life; to build upon the residual traditional Christianity that still lies deep in the background of the majority of families today, and to offer people both the challenge and the comfort of the gospel. In doing this he becomes vulnerable, as did Christ before him. But he proves himself a pastor after Christ's own heart, a faithful under-shepherd of the one true Shepherd whose love for the lost sheep is as great as for those within the fold. And in all his pastoral ministry, problems become opportunities and Christ is glorified.

---

[1] I am aware that many churches have women pastors. I use the male gender, throughout, not because of any male chauvinism but because it makes for an easier style and because men pastors are still in the majority!

[2] This article deals only with general home visiting — not the specialized ministries of hospital, industrial or prison visiting which present special problems and opportunities.

# Hospital Visiting

NORMAN AUTTON, M.A.

University Hospital of Wales, Cardiff

THE hospital visitor should be cognizant of the fact that he is, first and foremost, an ambassador of Christ, in whose name he ministers. He is not only the servant-bearer of the pastoral concern of the Christian community, but also the harbinger of the comfort and healing of the church's ministry to the sick and suffering. He is not at the bedside merely to give a cheery word, necessary as this might sometimes be. He is there for one reason only — to express by loving action the conviction that God is light, and that every good gift and every perfect gift is of the Father in whom there is no variation or shadow of turning. He is there to interpret or articulate to the patient what God is like, to mediate the reality of God's love. His message will arouse hope and proclaim the good news of the gospel — 'Come unto me all . . . whose load is heavy, and I will give you relief' (Mt 11[28]).

Personal prejudices and problems must be set aside so that he is free to concentrate on the patient as a person, and his whole attitude should be receptive as well as responsive. The key to hospital visiting is *empathy* which means the feeling of one personality into another until some state of identification is achieved. The wise visitor will 'diagnose' before he ministers, without any stereotyped approach or illusion of routine. His own personal prayers before visiting the wards will help him cultivate a sympathetic sensitivity to the needs and resources of those patients upon whom he is to call; his notebook of intercessions will be his constant companion, helping him to recognize their longings and prompting them to open their hearts. He will not be too anxious about 'techniques', what to say when, or what to respond should the patient say this or that. Indeed there will be many occasions when he will be ready to re-echo the words of Michel Quoist:

> This afternoon I went to see a patient at the hospital. From ward to ward I walked, through that city of suffering, sensing the tragedies hardly concealed by the brightly painted walls and the flower-bordered lawns. I had to go through a ward; I walked on tip-toe, hunting for my patient. My eyes passed quickly and discreetly over the sick, as one touches a wound delicately to avoid hurting. I felt uncomfortable, like the uninitiated traveller lost in a mysterious temple, like a pagan in the nave of a church. At the very end of the second ward I found my patient, and once there, I could only stammer. I had nothing to say.
>
> (*Prayers of Life* by Michel Quoist, Gill & Macmillan [1964], 65).

It will be essential to establish good working relationships with the ward staff, especially with the nursing officer and ward sister or charge-nurse. The latter's permission should always be sought before actual visits to patients are made. Constant liaison and cooperation with the hospital chaplain will also be necessary. Nothing is more frustrating than finding that the sick parishioner whom one has been so anxious to see is 'in theatre' on the very day one has chosen to visit, or that he or she has either been discharged or transferred to another hospital. It is important, too, that the minister always commends his members to the chaplain when they are admitted to the local hospital. The experienced visitor will not ask the patient about his condition or inquire from him what is wrong. The patient's illness is his own personal and private concern, and if he should wish the minister to know, he himself will tell him without being confronted with embarrassing questions. Neither will he ask the medical or nursing staff about the medical details of the patient for these too are highly confidential.

It is not so much a matter of knowing what to say or what to do, but how to feel alongside a sick brother at the bedside; how to feel with him and how to communicate this feeling to him. There can be no place in hospital visiting for text-book platitudes and pious clichés, because honesty, sincerity and genuineness must be its keynotes. To each sick person the gospel must mean the *good news*. As the minister sits at the bedside of the sick the very nature of man confronts him, his sickness and his health, his sinfulness and salvation, his brokenness and his wholeness. Each bedside visit becomes his testing ground. The very environment of the hospital will inevitably force him out of his detached shell into the very arena of life, to meet and struggle with life and death, guilt and estrangement, tragedy and triumph. On every side he will meet hurt bodies, injured spirits and distorted relationships. He will therefore need the utmost skill, self-discipline and watchfulness. He must needs be aware that shyness can often hinder or inhibit the introduction of spiritual matters when an opportune moment presents itself. He will be careful, too, not to allow his own personality to obtrude, but will rather see himself as a channel through which the family of Christ reaches out in love, concern and compassion to its sick members. In order to achieve this the minister himself has to come to terms with the problem of pain, suffering and death. The patient will often have to be helped to face up to the reality situation in which he finds himself, so that he neither minimizes its impact nor magnifies its seriousness.

Sickness is always more than the symptom and it will be necessary for the hospital visitor to be familiar with some of the emotional and spiritual factors in illness. It is a time of confusion and stress, often of childish fantasies and regressions. Sickness is a great leveller, for whatever the social or intellectual backgrounds of patients, in pyjamas all men are equal. The effects of being ill can be humiliating, embarrassing, and a threat to personal stability. There can be boredom, frustration and apprehension in a hospital ward, as well as a spirit of camaraderie and friendship. There are some folk who seem to thrive on hospital life, while others are so frightened and shocked that they seem almost incapable of communicating with doctors and nursing staff.

The first few moments of the pastoral call are of vital importance, for it is here that the visit is made or marred. There are three guiding principles — to look, to listen and to learn.

*To look:* The minister needs to be observant at the bedside, and will develop a keen sensitivity to meet the patient where he is. Who is this patient? How is he reacting to his illness? He will observe signs, postures, motions, expressions. Are there signs of fear behind the constant chatter? Is there depression masked by a false bravado? Is he relaxed and ready to talk, or is he tense and anxious? The minister should always look the sick person in the eye, not with an embarrassed gaze or frightening stare, but with a reassuring and sympathetic glance. Much can be learned from a patient's eyes, and a little of his character and something of his feelings can be gleaned.

*To listen:* Far too frequently the minister's call seems to open up with a barrage of questions — Where is the patient from? When did he come in? Has he had his operation? Does he have any visitors? Is he feeling better? Does he really get to know the patient in this way? Too frequent questioning implies the visitor stands opposite or over and against the patient rather than alongside. Most visitors become obsessed by words. 'Words, words, words. I'm sick of words . . . is that all you blighters can do?' The protest of Eliza in *My Fair Lady* must often be the unspoken thought of many a sick patient lying in a hospital bed at the mercy of an over-talkative minister. The most important question is not, 'What do I say to the patient?' but rather, 'What do I let the patient say to me?' Silence will often speak far more meaningfully than words, but it must not be the embarrassing silence of not knowing what to say. Rather is it the silence which knows exactly what to say but realizes that this is not the most opportune time to say it. Listening is something far more profound than merely keeping quiet while the other speaks. Active listening involves understanding, giving full attention not only to what the patient is *saying* but what he is *feeling*. This will allow the patient to give full expression to his inner feelings and his area of concern. Simon and Garfunkel in their song *The Sound of Silence* rightly complain of 'People talking without speaking, people hearing without listening'. Really to listen the minister must accept the other and care enough to give himself wholly to the other. Listening is active cooperation. By such empathizing the minister is symbolizing that he cares, is concerned, has time for the patient, is taking him seriously, is accepting him as a person. True listening is a wonderful source of reconciliation and healing.

*To learn:* Ministry to the sick is no one-way confrontation, but rather one of mutual understanding and growth. In ministering to the patient the pastor will be ministering to himself. There will be manifold lessons to be learnt if he is humble and open enough to perceive them. The sick have much to teach, and in many ways they are the 'givers' and we the 'receivers'. A ministry of reconciliation, of sharing and of true identification are among the hall-marks of pastoral care.

A true understanding of and appreciation for the patient's feelings will encourage conversation, and much will depend upon the minister himself being relaxed, comfortable, and secure at the bedside. The visit should commence as naturally as possible, and what information he may wish to receive from the patient will be acquired not so much from the asking of direct questions as from sympathetically listening to the spontaneous accounts of the patient. The visitor should phrase his own remarks in such a way as to make such forthcoming. By carefully observing and attentively listening he will be able to establish some degree of 'diagnosis' of the mental, emotional and spiritual needs of the patient, and to gauge his strengths and weaknesses.

There will often be a tendency to deliver 'sermonettes', or 'silver-lining' approaches, to give premature assurances or reassurances over which the minister has no authority, and to fall into the error of seeing his patient in terms of what he thinks he ought to be rather than recognizing him for what he is. The 'service' approach, 'What can I do for you, Mr A?', speaks to the insecurity of the visitor who obviously appears to be far more secure 'doing' things rather than 'being' in a creative relationship alongside the patient. A hospital visit becomes meaningful whenever there is humble willingness to be taught as well as to teach, to be guided as well as to guide. The minister's task will be to gain insight into the private world of the patient and look at the world through the patient's eyes. In this way he will be ministering to the whole person, in the totality of his sickness, in the reality situation in which he finds himself.

Too often can the hospital visitor see himself as a problem-solver or an advice-giver, an attitude which assumes that he knows best. To counsel means rather 'to deliberate together'. He will discreetly and sensitively feel the emotional pulse of the patient and discover thereby his emotional reaction to what is happening to him. It will be essential for the minister to remain neutral emotionally and yet avoid being coldly objective. The patient should be met on his own level with a warm responsiveness.

What is the best time to visit the hospital? Much will depend upon the circumstances and routine of the local hospital and the minister will need to exercise discretion. It is often wise to consult the ward staff beforehand and be guided by their suggestion. Meal times should always be avoided and morning visits are particularly unwelcome in the majority of wards. Visits to surgical patients should preferably be made in the afternoon or evening prior to the operation rather than the morning of the operation. Mid-afternoon or early evening visits are generally most appreciated.

Visits should always be kept brief and much will depend upon the physical condition of the sick member. Usually ten to fifteen minutes will be long enough. It is better to stay for a too-short period than to wear out your welcome. Should the patient be acutely ill the shorter the visit the better, but any sense of hurry or haste should be avoided. The length of the visit will be determined by observable cues.

There can be no hard and fast rules about when to pray at the bedside, and the minister will be wise to follow the needs and desires of the patient avoiding rigid rules of 'always' or 'never' praying. He must be open and receptive to the promptings of the Holy Spirit for 'There is no law dealing with such things as these' (Gal 5[22]). Sometimes the patient himself will ask the minister to pray, and when prayers are said they should be short, simple and direct, natural, informal and unobtrusive. 'I have heard a man offer a prayer for a sick person which amounted to a diagnosis followed by advice as to how God should treat the person', warns C. S. Lewis in *Letters to Malcolm: Chiefly on Prayer.*

The patient should be seen in the context of his family rather than as an isolated individual who happens to be sick. In a sense the members of his family are 'patients' too for they will often be tense, fearful and anxious. As one patient aptly described it: 'We're a closely knit family and when one of us is sick, we're all pretty sick'. In these days of unrestricted visiting periods the minister will frequently find members of the family at the bedside of the patient. Anxious and distressed families can be ministered to and comforted for they often welcome the very neutrality of one who has not been personally involved in the medical or nursing care of the patient. Should the minister be sent for in an emergency or 'sick-call' the fact that he has already seen or personally met the members of the family will enable him to take his place alongside them at the bedside in a far more meaningful way than if he were unknown to them. A stranger arriving on the scene at such a critical time can jar and disrupt, and create further tenseness and apprehension.

There should be no façade or pretence at the hospital bedside merely to win the approval and goodwill of the other, but rather a warm acceptance of the patient, feeling with him, thinking with him, and seeing him in the light of God's love. The patient has always to be met at his point of need. The minister may use all the verbal and practical techniques but unless he endeavours to enter with love, understanding, and compassion into the suffering and pain of the other, real and effective communication and relationship do not take place. Growth and healing can only be accomplished as a result of something behind and beyond the spoken word or practical deed, however well intentioned this may be. 'We saw his glory, such glory as befits the Father's only Son, full of grace and truth' (Jn 1¹⁴). Martin Buber sums it up rather wonderfully when he describes this warm-hearted relationship as 'experiencing the other side'.

All medical information known to the minister must be kept strictly confidential. Without thinking he can so easily and innocently divulge information which is officially private. Often well-intentioned and sympathetic fellow-members of his congregation will ask, 'I hear X is in hospital. What's wrong with him?'. He must never betray confidence and should respond courteously but evasively.

At the bedside the minister should avoid showing any alarm at 'drips' or any specialized equipment which may be about. It should be accepted as natural and normal, and it is always better to refrain from comment unless the patient first mentions it. An apprehensive attitude on the part of the visitor may make the patient feel sensitive and over-concerned about himself. It goes without saying of course that such equipment should never be tampered with or fingered.

In a hospital ward some patients become self-centred, difficult and petulant; others make their illness a means of gaining in understanding of and love for others. The minister must realize that by his art of gentleness and sensitivity he is often the one who determines which of these two attitudes the patient himself adopts. He will always bear in mind that the patient is host and he the visitor, the guest. He will be aware that sick people are highly sensitive to atmosphere and soon become disturbed by any signs of agitation and over-anxiety. By his quiet speech and attitude he will avoid the extremes of being apologetic for his presence on the one hand and over-boisterous in his approach on the other.

Hospital visiting is a testing ground of one's own spiritual life. The minister may use all the verbal and practical techniques, but unless he enters with love and compassion into the pain and suffering of the sick much of his ministry will be in vain. Illness can be a challenging and shattering experience. The minister will have no easy and slick answers to the various 'whys' and 'wherefores' and he must needs be rooted and grounded in a deep religious faith himself. 'When we brought you the gospel, we brought it not in mere words but in the power of the Holy Spirit, and *with strong conviction,* as you know well' (1 Thes 1[5]). There is no life situation like that of a hospital ward to put his faith to the test. He may have all the knowledge, wisdom and skill in the field of pastoral care, but if he has no real genuine love and concern for sick people it will profit him nothing. Hospital visiting calls for a life rooted in prayer, penitence and sacrament.

# Ministering to the Dying

GEOFFREY L. CLARK

Newcastle-upon-Tyne

MY ministry began in a small, run down Lancashire mill town. The people had suffered the depression of the '30s with its calamitous effects on the cotton industry; they knew about the pain of redundancy and rejection. The year was 1961, new hope had been created with light engineering and an entrepreneurial venture into the cheap domestic appliance market, and the economy was buoyant; then the light engineering cut back and the entrepreneur failed. Once again people were thrown out of work, once again there was anger, hurt and the frustration of helplessness. I was 24, I knew what the gospel had to say about the dignity of man and about the need for a just society. My instincts were to crusade.

Around that time I was introduced to FK (Fellowship of the Kingdom — a national fellowship composed mainly of Methodist ministers which meets in local groups for prayer, Bible study and fellowship). At an early meeting we engaged in discussion about the role of the ministry, in the course of which a man of middle years declared that twenty years earlier he had been told that the primary work of the minister was to prepare people to die. I recalled the words of Mr Wesley, who enjoined his preachers 'to preach as dying men to dying men', and heard what the brother was saying about the nature of our ministry, but nevertheless I exploded — the work of ministry was not to give substance to the communist joke about Christians offering pie in the sky but had more to do with the negro preacher's claim for 'jam where I am' — a proper life here with all that justice implied.

Twenty years on I still believe in and work for social justice but would not object to the claim about our primary aim quite so strongly. Dying people have taught me too much — people like Peggy who had as hard a death as anyone I have ever known. She took three years to die from a painful malignancy and through it all she was possessed of a serenity of spirit and an inner joy which welled up through her poor disfigured face. She didn't gain that from my ministry, but rather her faith and readiness for heaven was born and developed through many years of discipleship as in the fullness of her life she was 'prepared' to die.

This must be the first affirmation in anything I would share about ministry to the dying, that it does not begin on the death bed but rather commences in the Sunday School, where NT teaching about our heavenly citizenship, about the Christian Hope, about eternal life, are converted into songs which may be weak poetry and even trite theology but which allow assumptions on which later building can take place. To pursue this further would, however, be to escape the real intention of the editor in asking me to write about ministry to the dying, yet only when I make the assumption that death is a normal albeit unique part of life's experience can I attempt to describe some lessons learned about the specific area of ministry in the final stages of life.

Ministry to the dying is most possible when set in the context of a trusting relationship which allows the possibility of two people (the minister and the ministered to) to explore together their experience at that time. But, to be honest, as every pastor knows, it is usually not that simple. Sometimes he moves into a situation where he is hitherto unknown, at times the relationship to date has been of the casual greetings and occasionally even of hostility; nevertheless with patent compassion and patient care he must seek to build a relationship in which to work.

In some societies dying and death are honoured — the family gather round for a solemn farewell and the final blessing is given by the old warrior or dying mother. In ours we treat it rather as our Victorian grandparents treated sex — as a necessary though unseemly part of life which should never be discussed. The process is often so overlaid with the games people play to protect their loved ones from the truth that the pastor can find that he is walking through a 'playground' of 'white lies' — falsely 'happy' deceit. The games start with a modern, though widely accepted folk belief, that it's better for people 'not to be told'. I have tried to understand the reasons for this and can only think that, as it often starts with the doctor's advice, it is as much about his wish not to distress or upset his patient as about a twentieth-century agnosticism. However, whatever its genesis, it can easily turn the playground into a minefield with all the consequent danger and pain. This is to be faced and then combatted and the pastor is in a strong position to do this.

I am persuaded that we must above all encourage openness. This does not mean a cold and crude statement given to the dying person that he has six months to live — though that information may well have to be shared. It does mean being willing to share feelings and information and help individuals and families to a point where they can truly help each other face the mutual pain of parting and strengthen one another through it, at times maybe absorbing their frustration and anger with God about its unfairness.

Let me introduce Bill and Betty who are a typical example of a situation familiar to most. In their late fifties and childless they were looking forward to retirement and the opportunities of expanding their life together through learning and through service. Betty became ill. She had a hysterectomy and for a time was better. They went away for a holiday, but whilst away she became ill again. The holiday was shortened and they returned home. The doctor visited, a hospital appointment arranged, Betty was reassured that all was well — just complications which would clear with proper treatment. They were both relieved — until the next day, when Bill received a telephone message that the doctor wanted to see him privately. He knew before he went what he would hear — his wife's condition was serious, she had an inoperable condition and only a few weeks to live. 'I don't think there is any need for her to know — just make her last days as happy as possible', he was advised.

Bill did not tell Betty about the phone call or the interview, though he did tell some of her family who reinforced the doctor's advice. He accepted that advice. They had had a good marriage and he wanted the best for her. But then the inevitable happened: Betty's condition deteriorated. She asked some half questions and found evasive answers or a hearty reassurance. Soon a 'no go' area developed in their conversation and new tensions were set up. They had in the past supported each other at every crisis, sharing joys and fears; now, when they needed each other most, they were unable to share their deepest needs — of open, accepting, supporting love — and Bill needed Betty's help as much as she needed his. They needed to help each other for, as the marriage service says, this is part of what marriage is about, and they were prevented from giving that help, so that their marriage ended in a lack of openness which had never before characterized it.

Ministry to such people means spending time, listening, sitting in silence, just being available — encouraging them to talk of their fears, hopes and questions. Perhaps for a time interpreting the couple to each other, helping them to become free, free to love openly and share, to weep together and comfort one another. The questions asked arise from the most natural fears and it helps to share them. Some are entirely medical — about the changes in the body, the help available when pain intensifies. Others are very practical — about provision for the dependants, especially when the man is dying. There are the frustrations and anger needing to be expressed, and the questions about life after death. Ministry means allowing these and other questions to be opened up, for they can become windows into the soul, as it were, so that healing light can shine in.

Many fears are expressed. I gather them together under these heads:

*The fear of not knowing.* This results in questions which are only occasionally expressed and at certain times — wondering how one will cope with the days and experiences ahead, arising out of observation at the dying in others and uncertainty of one's own capacity to bear what lies in the future.

There is *the fear of being alone.* We know that those who are to be bereaved will mourn and have to be helped through, but mourning is also a part of the experience of the dying. He is going to be cut off from people he loves and depends on, and the anticipation of the separation is as painful for both. Coupled with this is the very isolation that sickness brings. We all know how wretched and isolated we feel when, for example, we suffer an attack of vomiting. The dying person can feel quite alone and be frightened by the experience. Physical reassurance in ministry which accompanies the words, and can be a touch, a hand held, or the laying on of hands can all form a part of the pastor's response.

Alongside these is the *fear of losing human dignity.* Miss

Smith whose manners have been impeccable and whose standards were created by the dignity of her background had a stroke; she could no longer eat cleanly, she became incontinent and her memory became uncertain. Having known Miss Smith and seen the deterioration in her condition the fear of becoming like that can be a terrible trial.

The pastor is not amongst the prophets and the questions which reveal these fears cannot all be answered, but his ministry is not in providing answers but rather in being a priest; that is in building a bridge or revealing the bridge between God and man for the comfort and hope of the dying. This will be done not through accomplished techniques but in giving time and being willing maybe to be there, sitting maybe in silence and thus meeting the great need of someone to share, to accept and understand. Ours is not to fill every moment with words, be they of the most pious type — it is an occupational hazard that parsons can be terrible talkers — instead we go to represent a quality of care and love which brought the universe into being and which even now surrounds each needy soul.

Looking back I have found very little fear or even thought of meeting God in many people to whom I have talked. This may, indeed, speak rather more about today's preaching and teaching; it may speak of deep faith, or the lack of it. Plainly it is hardly appropriate to regard a sick bed as a prison in which one can evangelize a captive audience and one must always be sensitive to the wishes of the sick, yet, nevertheless, there is at times a willingness, if not eagerness, to discuss the meaning of life, and a concern far greater than curiosity to talk and learn about eternal life and heaven. We fail our Lord and our fellows if we do not share our convictions and his promises, for in these is hope.

I would suggest that our ministry is fulfilled in this sharing of God's fatherly love. Three ways in which this is done effectively are through the reading of scriptures, prayer, and sharing communion. The familiar biblical passages have been known and loved since childhood. This very familiarity is a comfort and a reminder of the unchanging, and in the final days of life can give great support. At times I read from the patient's own Bible, and will read aloud even if he is apparently unconscious. I offer prayer in the same way, making short and simple affirmations of faith and thanksgiving. How often have we been told of the comatosed man or woman saying 'Amen' after such a prayer. We know that hearing often remains when other senses are dim, which stands as both a warning and an opportunity in ministry. Sharing the last rites of the church is not part of the tradition of the church in which I have grown, yet the opportunity of sharing communion with the dying should not be lightly dismissed, for in it is symbolized all that we would say or have to offer, and Protestants ought to give more weight to this I believe.

Our first aim is to unite a dying man with his own family and loved ones, encouraging them to share the pain and supporting them through it, after making that pain one's own. 'Do not become emotionally involved', some will say to the young minister. I know no ministry which is not costly to the minister through his involvement, and whilst some detachment will be retained, love given will cost a great deal and should not be withheld.

The second aim is to make him feel a part of mankind — that suffering is set into the context of life, and that he is still a part of the world which goes on outside the window. And even in extremity he contributes something towards the race.

Thirdly, one hopes it will help a man to feel more fully a part of the church of Christ, not just through the sacrament and the prayers of the church but through a growing awareness of the nature of the church triumphant with which he is in communion.

Principally however this ministry has the aim of helping the dying man to know that Christ is on the way with him. The greatest lesson I have learned is that ministry is not 'one way', for the dying have ministered to me as much as I have ministered to them, and that's no new lesson. I will always thank God for Peggy mentioned earlier who shortly before the end asked if we would sing in church the hymn, 'How blessed is life if lived for Thee' with its remarkable verse:

> All day to walk beneath Thy smile,
>   Watching Thine eyes to guide me still,
> To rest at night beneath Thy care,
>   Guarded by Thee from every ill.

Nor will I forget George, my Church Treasurer, with whom I talked ten days before his death on a particularly bad day for him. He was not an articulate Christian; his language was that of accounts and he kept the church's to the glory of God. On that occasion I simply said to him, 'It's hard George', and he replied, 'Aye, but the love of Jesus is sure and will see me through!' It is from people like these that I have learned about ministry. Others have no doubt learned more and given more, but what I have I share.

# The Pastor and the Young Fundamentalist

JAMES B. BATES, B.A.

Southlands College, Wimbledon

THE Shorter Oxford English Dictionary makes fundamentalism sixty years old this year. It defines it as: 'Strict adherence to traditional orthodox tenets (e.g., the literal inerrancy of Scripture) held to be fundamental to the Christian faith'. This allows it many interpretations and forms so that it is easier to talk about characteristics rather than specific beliefs. As a conscious theological position it appears to have developed as a reaction to the theories of science and the critical study of the Bible. Much of the debate over fundamentalism, therefore, centres on the nature of scripture, and the differing views on this tend to separate fundamentalists from other Christians.

To approach fundamentalists with arguments about scripture is equivalent to a declaration of war. Anyone attempting to 'enlighten' the fundamentalist is regarded either with suspicion as an enemy attacking a cherished belief or as someone in need of help. The pastor is tempted to regard the fundamentalist as someone with a problem, but for the fundamentalist there is no problem. He is not a seeker after the truth or salvation, he has found it. It is the other members of the church and possibly the pastor himself who are in error.

Most Christian communities are willing to tolerate a certain latitude of opinion and even of belief. Creative discussion is possible and people can learn from each other, but with fundamentalists there is no need for questioning except as inquiry into revealed truth. It is a characteristic of many fundamentalist speakers that they do not invite open discussion at the end of their addresses. People may come and inquire from the speaker after the meeting, but more as seekers after enlightenment than debaters challenging opinions. Controversy is not welcomed and yet fundamentalist groups often cause controversy and divisions within Christian communities, whether they are churches or colleges.

Fundamentalism also poses a problem for the church because it is attractive to the young and especially to the young in higher education. In universities and colleges the more fundamentalist groups such as Christian Unions (now often called Christian Fellowships) are strongly supported while the Student Christian Movement and other more 'liberal' Christian groups struggle for survival. Why is it that students, who are encouraged to examine and question beliefs and opinions, so often turn to fundamentalism? There is no clear answer, but it does seem that at a critical time of life fundamentalism provides an answer to an insoluble problem and therefore an emotional security.

Most of us find ourselves perplexed by the mysteries of existence and the student even more so because in many cases he is forced by his studies to face issues which are deeply disturbing. Many take refuge in some kind of agnosticism. If no one can be certain about anything, there is room for hope. Only the thorough-going atheist will force himself to 'build on unyielding despair'. Some young people turn to fundamentalism as an escape. It offers certainty in an uncertain world. Others, however, turn to it because it offers an alternative view of the world which, within its own terms, makes sense of their experience. They begin with the concept of God as they understand him from their reading of the Bible and work out a cosmology from that. They see attempts to understand God through nature and reason as wasted effort and lack of faith in the revealed truth of the Bible. They find evidence for their beliefs in the success of the evangelical churches in Britain, the growth of the Pentecostal churches overseas and the survival of the persecuted Christians in the Communist world. They look for evidence of God at work in the events of the world and in answer to prayer in their own lives. They tend to take miracle as supernatural intervention and expect to see God providing for them, guiding them and changing people's lives.

These characteristics are deeply disturbing to those who feel more at home with an interpretation of the faith which is more closely related to human understanding and experience, yet all these feature in scripture and have been characteristics of revival movements which have in the long run enriched and extended the church. The evangelical zeal of fundamentalists can be divisive because some turn their attention to practising members of the church, but they also challenge and win those with no church background. Many young people have become fundamentalist because it was through fundamentalists that they first came to know of the gospel.

Many of us may not be able to share the cruder expectations of the fundamentalists but they challenge us to consider our own Christian witness and commitment. The stress on the authority of the Bible calls us not only to understand it but to live by it. The emphasis on miracle forces us to think out again how God is working in his world. The Pentecostal, or charismatic, element makes us reconsider the resources that are ours. The evangelical zeal calls us to our own responsibility for mission and to witness.

The wider church community has much to offer in return, an ecumenical spirit, a social and political concern, an appreciation of the value of the natural and human, and an understanding of God that comes through art, learning and science. The separation of these two approaches must be prevented, since each has so much to give the other and both share the same fundamental faith. Young fundamentalists must be shown that they belong to a community which values them and their contribution even if it may not agree with all they say or do. In this the pastor has a key role. The following suggestions come from a long experience as residential chaplain to a mainly residential college with a strong Christian Union (now calling itself Christian Fellowship) as well as other Christian groups. It is a privileged position which not every pastor or chaplain may have, but what follows is born of experience and may prove helpful to others working in different situations, but facing similar problems.

(a) The pastor should aim to attend the meetings of the CU or similar group as regularly as he attends those groups which are closer to his own way of thinking. He goes as a listener to discover at first hand what speakers say and what the groups do. He goes to share as far as he can in the fellowship of the groups. At times he will find things said and done which conflict with his ideas and approach, but he is not there to criticize or to comment, unless his opinion is asked. It is unlikely that he will be invited to speak, but his presence will be appreciated. He will come to know the group as people and discover them as individuals, each with distinctive attitudes and beliefs. In winning their confidence he may be in a position to help them if they need to turn to him and he will be in a position to assist those who, like him, question some of the things said or done. Above all he will find that he is challenged personally by much he hears and sees. In the life of the group and in their interpretation of scripture he will be made to reconsider many things which the church has neglected. As mutual understanding grows so the link with the church community will be maintained and strengthened.

(b) The pastor must be ready to invite people from the fundamentalist groups to share in the religious life of the community, whether it be church or college. This can be disturbing since some will use the opportunity to impose their own opinions and methods on those who may not appreciate them. The pastor, however, is there to pick up the pieces and to build up understanding. The fundamentalist speaker may cause a certain amount of distress, but can also provoke serious conversation which breaks through the reserve which prevents so many church members from talking about their faith.

Team preaching appeals to many young people and this can help them to a deeper and broader understanding of the faith. In group preparation extreme and unreal ideas can be modified as biblical material is studied and as the service is planned. The pastor or leader of the team can guide the thinking, though it would be unwise for him always to insist on his own ideas and opinions. There is an art in taking young people's ideas, however crude, and helping them to develop them without taking them over. If young fundamentalists find that they can work alongside the pastor or other church members trust will grow, and as they share in leading worship they will feel both recognized and respected. The pastor must be ready to take full responsibility for what may happen or what may be said in such services, but he will defend the right of the young people to make their contribution to worship and turn criticism into constructive discussion. In most cases congregations will show understanding and appreciation of what the young people aim to do, even if there are things that are hard to accept. Public worship, especially in the larger churches, is hardly the place for young people to make their contribution if it is likely to be controversial. Great care must be taken to find the right congregation or meeting and people who will be supportive and sympathetic.

(c) The Sacrament of Holy Communion provides a meeting place for Christians of all shades of belief within a Christian community, whether college or church. If the pastor or chaplain has built up a good relationship with the fundamentalist group then he may find himself invited to celebrate Communion with them. He may not be invited to preach, but his role as the celebrant will be respected. Similarly the pastor can invite groups to take part in Communion by sharing in the administration by reading lessons or taking prayers. In both cases the unity of shared activity transcends differences of opinion and emphasizes the central beliefs we all hold together.

(d) Wherever possible the pastor or chaplain should share in Bible study with the young fundamentalists. They may not come to the Bible study courses he has planned, but that is no reason why he should not go to theirs. Again, he goes primarily to listen, to discover what they are thinking, to find out how they approach the Bible, and to share as much as he can in their aims. As confidence between them grows he will be able to show them how important it is to ask such questions as, 'Who wrote the documents?' 'How did they come to be written? — and when?' and, 'For what purpose were they written?' He will be able to point out how misleading it can be to quote texts out of context and that often there are parallel traditions which can help with interpretation. Too often young fundamentalists are introduced to doctrinal arguments based on texts before they have come to understand the nature of scripture or the circumstances in which it was written. They need to be shown that biblical scholarship deepens understanding and faith and clarifies what is often bewildering.

It is important that the pastor acquaint himself with the more recent publications of the IVF and other publishers who consider themselves as conservative. He will find that they have taken critical scholarship into account even if they are guarded about many of its conclusions. The aim of the pastor is not to win the young fundamentalist over to his point of view but to help him to gain all he can from those who share the fundamentalist approach to the faith. To do this the pastor must study conservative writing at its best.

In shared Bible study the pastor may be able to reveal the human aspect of the Bible — that it was written by people like us for people with needs similar to our own. He will show how the experiences of the people of the Bible can help us to understand our own and that they only came to faith by questioning the traditions of their day. This may encourage the young fundamentalist to question for himself and find a personal and more human approach to the faith.

(e) Fundamentalists are sometimes known as Conservative Evangelicals and evangelism is one of their prime concerns. This can take the form of proselytizing and causing distress to young people by insisting that theirs is the only way to salvation, but their evangelical zeal is a challenge to the church which too often has made little or no attempt to witness beyond it own community. If the enthusiasm of young fundamentalists can be channelled into the general witness of the church both will gain from the experience. In a number of college missions I have found that fundamentalist students have worked happily in a team with other students. They lived on church premises together, catering for themselves and sharing in whatever work the church gave them to do. They visited, leafleted in the streets, spoke in the open air, shared in house and fellowship groups and took part in youth work. Prayer and Bible study were linked to specific activities and situations. They met church members and discovered how, as Christians, they coped with the situations facing them. In every way their faith was related to real circumstances. In meeting people of all kinds and in attempting to communicate with them they became more human in their faith, and in working with other Christians they came to appreciate that there could be more than one approach to the faith. The churches benefited from the energy, enthusiasm and conviction of the students.

(f) Not every church community can find ways of providing this kind of experience for their young people, but they can be encouraged to share in community service or social work of some kind. There was a time, not so long ago, when fundamentalists were very critical of the 'social gospel' and 'do-gooders'. There was the naïve belief that if people were converted then society would automatically be redeemed, or that the troubles of the world were evidence of God's judgment on the world and that the mission of Christians was to save people from it. This is no longer the case. The conservative wing of the church has rediscovered a tradition of social concern that can be traced back to the Evangelicals of the early nineteenth century who made such great contributions to the reform movements of their day. CUs may not put social problems on their programme of public meetings, but I find them very ready to discuss moral, social and political problems. They are ready to be involved in community service and are not indifferent to the concerns of the Student Union. Over the years they have provided their share of its officers.

Community service, like involvement in mission, can widen and humanize the faith of young fundamentalists. Extreme fundamentalism can become very inhuman and unrelated to life. The image of God is forbidding, the image of human nature is arid, and people are seen as significant only in terms of a rigid soteriology. Love is widely quoted, but the objects of love are carefully selected. This is fundamentalism at its worst and is not true of many who call themselves fundamentalist, but if we recognize this as a tendency in fundamentalism then we can best help fundamentalist young people, not by trying to argue them out of their beliefs, but by developing their beliefs through encouraging them to work for and to meet people. By meeting people and working with them — the elderly, children, the handicapped and socially deprived — and by seeing how they respond to life they will come to appreciate the humanity God has created in those about them and in themselves.

(g) Finally, the pastor is very soon aware that fundamentalists tend to have very definite ideas about who is and who is not a Christian. They draw a circle around the community of faith so that any one outside it feels excluded. Many speakers I have heard play on this and can have a very disturbing effect upon young people who are growing up in the faith. Most Christian communities expect some kind of recognizable response in their young people, but fundamentalists tend to be very specific in their expectations, not giving much room for individuality. Sometimes one is confronted either by young people brought up in the faith, baptized and confirmed, who claim that they have only just become Christians, or by other similar young people who have been told that they are not. In both cases one can be grateful that the young person has been challenged about belief and come to realize that it demands a personal decision. In the former case, while one is glad that they have come to a new awareness of the faith and one encourages them to explore the meaning of that experience, there will be a time when they need to be reminded that their becoming a Christian has been a long process in which many people have played a part over the years, their parents, their teachers and the church of their childhood. In the latter case, while reassuring the young person that not everyone has to conform to a specific requirement, the pastor will help him to work out his own response to the faith. The fundamentalist, for all he may resent him and reject his rigidity, has made him see that the Christian faith is not something which can be taken for granted although it is granted freely to us by God.

Two requirements can cause difficulties for many young people. One is believer's baptism and the other is baptism by the Holy Spirit. This is not the place to go into the theology of either of these. The former creates difficulties for those brought up within a paedobaptist tradition. They are deeply impressed by the baptism of their friends and infant baptism seems meaningless in comparison. I have never been very successful in persuading any of my own young people who have been set on a second baptism to give it up, but I have been grateful that they have come to discuss the issue with me. For many of them it has been the first time that anyone has shown them how fully infant baptism represents the truth of the gospel. A few years ago I found a number of young fundamentalists very disturbed because, although they claimed to be converted and baptized Christians, they were told that they had to be baptized by the Holy Spirit and that they should be able to show evidence of the same in their lives. While one tried to free them from the rigid interpretations that had been given to them, one was grateful for the opportunity to explore the ways in which the Holy Spirit works in our lives.

Again and again the fundamentalist calls us back to consider the fundamentals of the faith. We may not interpret those fundamentals in the same way, and he may be a disturbing influence in the church, but it will be to our loss, as well as his, if the church becomes divided. We should remember that if he does leave the church he will take many young people with him.

# Part IV
# The Daily Round

# The Pastor and His Family

GRAHAM A. PATRICK, B.A., B.D., Ph.D.

Alsager

A STORY has long circulated in clerical circles about a man who has just retired from the ministry, sitting down with his wife to look at the family photograph album. She shows him one particular photograph of the family on holiday. He points to two children who are in the picture, and says: 'But darling, who are those children?' and she replies solemnly: 'They are yours, my dear!' The story grossly exaggerates the point, of course. But for many ministers it will touch a raw nerve, and highlight one of the principal areas of conflict and tension within their lives — the struggle between loyalty to their work and their family. It is a struggle unknown to the celibate priest, but for those in the post-Reformation, non-celibate tradition it is a source of continual tension, something with which ministers are constantly trying to come to terms. Certain features of contemporary life, moreover, have made the problem more acute than ever in recent years.

In this article we shall look at some of the reasons for this conflict and consider how it may be resolved. The intention of the Editor is that contributors to this series should offer practical advice from personal experience. I am a male minister and can only write from that perspective. The problems for the woman minister may be very different, and I would not feel competent to consider these.[1]

One of the major problems faced by a minister's family is the *invasion of its privacy*. The manse or the vicarage is not simply a private home. It is an 'open house' for the neighbourhood, and the minister's office. The telephone may ring, and people may call, at all hours of the day or night. Meals are frequently interrupted by one or the other. There cannot be many clergy, however dedicated, who have not sometimes longed to be private citizens rather than public figures, able to enjoy the privacy and relative anonymity of an ordinary family.

In recent years, more and more ministers have tried to make things easier for themselves and their families by separating their home from their work as far as possible, and having an office and telephone at the church. It is my experience that although this may be helpful in some respects, it does not really remove the pressure from the manse. The minister does not work a 'nine to five' day, and so it is presumed by most people that he will be at home in the evening, which is when the family are also at home.

Another factor affecting family life is the *difficulty of having 'time off'*. This is a problem familiar to clergy of all denominations. Because of the nature of their calling, they are often over-conscientious, and because their work is by its nature never completed, many clergy work impossibly long hours. In modern jargon, a good proportion of ministers and priests are 'workaholics'. It is not unusual to find men who regularly work a sixty to seventy hour week. The so-called 'leisure revolution' has yet to affect this profession, it seems! This, inevitably, has a profound effect upon a minister's family life. I recall one reminiscence by a son of the manse, speaking of his father when he (the son) was a boy: 'He was always in his study. We never saw him.' Children, especially when young, come to resent having a father who never has time to play or relax with them. It is no easier for the wife. It is difficult to find uninterrupted time together, except late at night, and then an overworked minister is often too exhausted to listen to his wife's problems. 'You have time for everyone except me!' is a complaint which has humbled many a minister!

Bishops, Moderators and Chairmen of Districts are putting much more stress today upon the importance of their clergy having adequate leisure and time for their families. This is a welcome emphasis, but the nature of a minister's job means that it will always be a problem. In particular, there is the fact that for most people in the community the weekend is a family time, whereas for the clergy it cannot be so.

A third factor is *the position of the minister's wife.* On the one hand, there is the widespread assumption that she will be a kind of 'curate', involved in the life of the church as President of the Women's Fellowship, and so on. This is something clergy wives have always had to recognize. Many have been happy to accept this role, others have repudiated it. Today, there is a very strong rebellion, especially amongst younger wives, against this expectation. The Women's movement is largely responsible for this. It is widely accepted now that a woman has as much right to a career as a man. Therefore, many ministers' wives have careers of their own and object strongly to the assumption that they should be alongside their husbands in the official work of the church. As far as their commitment to the church is concerned, they see their main role as being a support to their husband, holding the family together, rather than any particular involvement in the life of the church.

Closely connected with all this is the feeling of the minister's wife that she is not treated by the congregation as a person in her own right. She is 'the minister's wife'. This is a problem faced by the wives of many professional people, of course, but it is a bone of contention today with many younger wives, influenced by the changed status of women within our society.

Then, fourthly, we may briefly mention *finance*. Ministers vary greatly in their attitudes to this, and in their ability or inability to manage on their stipend. One point of view is set out in a later chapter. What must be said, however, is that it is frequently a source of tension within the pastor's family. Many clergy find that however hard they try, they cannot manage on their stipend. This means that either the wife must go out to work, whether she wishes to do so or not, or the minister himself must do something additional to bring in extra income, which puts him and the family under considerable extra pressure. In either case, resentment can build up within the family against the circumstances which have led to this. It must be said, however, that clergy families are in no way alone in facing this problem today. And the chapter referred to provides a number of very helpful practical suggestions as to how to come to terms with life on a clergy stipend.

Finally, there is the *mobility factor*. This affects clergy of some denominations much more than others. Methodists are particularly vulnerable since they move, on the average, every five to seven years. All will know, however, what a disturbing influence moving house can have upon family life. Children are taken away from friends, and education is disrupted. It is not unknown today for wives to refuse to move with their husbands because they wish to retain their job. In fairness, however, it must be said that clergy are by no means the only group to experience this problem. It is one shared with several other very mobile professions (e.g., bank managers and the armed services).

These, then, are some of the factors which give rise to conflict and tension within the minister's family. It may seem that we have painted an unnecessarily negative picture. It is important, however, to be aware of the wide range of pressures operating upon a minister's family life.

This is all the more pertinent when it is acknowledged that marriage problems and breakdown amongst clergy have greatly increased in recent years. Bishops, Chairmen of Districts and Moderators would testify to their concern at this, and the fact that an increasing amount of their time is given to counselling and supporting clergy families where breakdown is threatened or has actually taken place. In the light of this, we do well to take seriously the particular situation of the minister's family, and the peculiar pressures working upon it at this time.

Now, it must be said at this point that, of course, there is another aspect of the picture. We must acknowledge that marriage and family life can, in itself, be of great enrichment to the work of a minister. It is wrong to think of the relationship only in terms of tension. Most married clergy are frequently aware of the new dimension which family life adds to their work. In counselling and preaching, the married minister is at a great advantage because he knows at first hand the joys and sorrows of married life, the challenge and possibilities brought by children, and the various stages in the evolution of family life. He knows it from his own experience and this adds immensely to his authority within the life of the church. The letter to the Hebrews lays great emphasis upon the fact that since Christ has fully entered into our human condition, he is able to help us in our struggle with our human nature. There is something analogous to this in the position of the married clergyman.

It would be wrong, too, to dwell entirely upon the negative effect of life in the manse or vicarage upon children. It is undoubtedly true to say that children gain a great deal from growing up in such an environment. While they certainly sometimes see the less acceptable face of the church, they also gain a great deal from living in different parts of the country (or even the world), from meeting a wide range of people, and from the very varied and interesting pattern of life going on around them in the manse or vicarage.

It must be said, therefore, that it would be quite incorrect to see a minister's family life entirely in terms of a 'problem' to be overcome. What equally needs saying, however, is that nothing is gained by glossing over problems and tensions which undoubtedly exist, and which are an everyday reality for many clergy families.

We must look, finally, at ways of coping with the pressures outlined earlier. They are all in some sense inseparable from the nature of the work the pastor does, and so they are not likely to 'go away'. He has to learn to live with them and to take a positive attitude towards them.

Most important of all would seem to be the need for the pastor to order his life, so that within his daily and weekly timetable there is 'family time' written in, so to speak. This means taking time-off each day to be at leisure with the family. This will involve protecting meal-times which are an important focus of family life. There ought to be at least one meal in the day when the telephone will be unanswered or taken off the hook, because the family needs to be at leisure together. It is not possible for the pastor to be totally available and at the same time to preserve his sanity and the quality of his family life. It means also taking regular time-off each week, having a 'family-day' when as far as possible the only demands upon him are the demands of his family. My wife has sometimes remarked, when we are setting off with the children on a day out: 'Are you really *ours* today?'

What is vital is to recognize that this kind of pattern cannot be achieved without planning ahead. The pastor needs to mark his time-off in his diary just as meetings and other parish commitments are marked in. There must be an attempt to lead an ordered life if the family is to be given the time and attention it merits.

The other pressing need seems to be for some system of pastoral care to be organized for the pastor's family. In the past it has been assumed that this was his responsibility, but in recent years it has been increasingly recognized that this must come from outside the family. We have mentioned earlier the pressures upon a minister's wife to conform to an imposed pattern. She is sometimes a very lonely figure if she is not the type to be involved in traditional church meetings. It is possible for a church to be very concerned about pastoral care and yet to ignore completely the pastoral care of the minister's family. This kind of insensitivity is by no means as uncommon as it should be. Our congregations need much more encouragement to see the care of the minister's family — and, indeed, the minister — as an important part of their pastoral responsibility. The alternative is for the pastor to ask one of his ministerial colleagues specifically to exercise pastoral care of his family. Since most clergy today have a very heavy pastoral load, it would seem that the most fruitful way forward is the recognition of the vital role of the laity in relation to the pastor's family.

The pastor also needs to listen sometimes to what his lay people are saying. One of the turning-points in my own ministry came when one of the members of my congregation in Liverpool said to me, after I had been preaching about marriage and family life: 'You know, you have no right to talk to us about family life unless you yourself are giving time to your own family'. It was a remark which brought me face to face with myself and my own priorities. It convinced me once and for all that, however hard a minister is working, if he is sacrificing his family to his work, his priorities are wrong.

---

[1] I attempted to secure an article on 'The Woman Minister' but met with the response that women ministers regard themselves simply as 'ministers', so that the subject would be inappropriate.—EDITOR.

# Pastors and Colleagues

CHRISTOPHER P. BURKETT, B.A.

Harlescott, Shrewsbury

As a prospective ordinand I was invited to a local clergy meeting to observe what went on. To my dismay I discovered that amongst this group of 'professional Christians' competition, tension, and dispute was rife. In my youthful naïveté I assumed that people who shared a common calling to the ordained ministry would inevitably work well together, unhindered by the usual misunderstandings and tensions common in other walks of life. Whereas, in fact, those difficulties may be worse amongst ministers because of the highly individualistic model of working still prevalent in the ordained ministry of our churches. Any meeting of comparatively recently appointed ministers will always produce a crop of people who have had unfortunate experiences with senior colleagues. The curate's egg is far from wholly good! And many efforts in shared ministry founder when the enthusiasm of the initiators is no longer there.

This article is written in the conviction that the pastor working totally alone, or with no more than a vague commitment to a wider grouping, is no longer an adequate model of practice (if it ever was). And further, that closer cooperation with a colleague can provide the essential stimulus and support necessary for effective ministry today. I have in mind two or three ministers working together, rather than specially constituted teams with their own particular problems. Perhaps the most common of such relationships is that of vicar and curate, or minister and assistant, though similar considerations apply to paid lay-workers and specialist ministers attached to local congregations. That said, the possibility of working much closer with a colleague may be a very beneficial option that local ministers alone could take up informally.

The importance of what is put into the first contacts and the early days of working together cannot be over stressed. If a minister is joining an already well established senior colleague, time in the initial visits spent on the discussion of overall plans and policies for the churches served will be well used. This is more valuable than rushing around trying to introduce the newcomer to office holders, community leaders and the like, which will come later. Where it is possible for the incoming minister to visit Sunday services, preferably not as an officiant, this will be valuable in gauging 'the feel' of the people he is coming to, but not as an opportunity of getting to know individuals. As so little is remembered when visiting a new environment it is best to concentrate initially on the ministers themselves, their plans for working, and their hopes of their churches and their relationship. All the other vital introductions can be made slowly in the first months of working together when they are more likely to be remembered. Like considerations apply to geography and place names. How many new pastors have had to allow themselves an extra hour for a funeral service because the location of the crematorium had been shown them many months before when there had been too many other things to consider!

The newcomer needs to be assured that there is a place for his or her ministry. The first months can be very disheartening if the impression is given that everything is already being done, every job is occupied, and there is nothing new under the sun. The willingness to share must be evident from the first, and the senior colleague may well have to give way to his new assistant in some areas. A specific, large task for the newcomer to work at can be a great help, for example, a complete revision of the visiting lists. Both colleagues are likely to have quite definite expectations about each other, each one's particular roles, and how they will function together. These things are often left unsaid or at best simply assumed, when they need to be made explicit if troubles are to be avoided. A good way of achieving this is the drawing up of an agreed contract between the colleagues, meant purely for their own use. It is best if this contract is deliberately written out and not left as a purely verbal agreement. It should include such matters as areas of responsibility, commitments of prayer, worship and study, procedures for day to day pastoral work, arrangements for preaching and leading of worship, strong and weak points of each other's ministry, particular areas of work needing time spent on them, covering for days-off and holidays — in fact anything that appertains to the working relationship. The initial contract may need to be revised quite quickly, but after that it should be put to one side for twelve months or so, and then used for reassessment and the re-ordering of priorities. Many ministers I am sure will be reluctant to undertake such a contract because it seems so time consuming, formal, and demanding of a degree of frankness that we sometimes shy away from. In practice, however, it yields extremely positive benefits in terms of learning, assessing goals and priorities, and overcoming difficulties, and is consequently well worth the effort and time involved.

So far I have concentrated on the relationship of the ministers themselves as it is surely essential that this should begin on a sure footing, but the relationship of the ministers to their congregations also needs consideration. In today's circumstances of economic stringency no doubt the financial requirements to provide for more than one minister will have inevitably been discussed at length. It is vital that lay members be convinced of the pastoral, worship, and missionary advantages of another member of staff. Comments like, 'We're a training parish, that's why he's here', or, 'Her real job is in the schools, she only comes to us for Sundays', not only illustrate confusion about the assistant's role but may be extremely hurtful. I recently heard of members of one congregation who were perplexed as to what use the curate with a doctorate, who was arriving the following week, could possibly be to them. Congregations need to be carefully prepared in teaching and discussion for the arrival of another minister. It is not only in Free Church circles that the question will arise as to whether with training and encouragement local lay people might not assume the assistant's role. It is to be hoped that such preparation as takes place would be part of the continuing examination of the ministry of all God's people in that locality.

Local church ministry is still widely viewed as a one man (or woman) show. 'It was only the curate who came, not the vicar', is still often heard. This is an attitude hard to break down even in churches used to having more than one pastor. Perhaps it is best tackled by the ministers themselves making it obvious that each one of them takes the lead in different areas according to circumstances and ability. For example, the senior colleague should resist the temptation always to take the funerals of long-standing church members, since this is liable to reinforce the impression that the assistant is somehow a second-best minister. On the other hand, the assistant must also avoid creating new areas of work which come to be seen as his preserve alone, something which often happens in the church's ministry to young people. The dilemma is that between each minister having particular areas of responsibility and their sharing of responsibility in all areas. Sometimes hard to resolve issues of status and seniority between the ministers must be dealt with if their partnership is to function well. My own feeling is that an open sharing of responsibility is to be preferred, which is likely also to encourage lay people to take their part. By careful planning this can be achieved without unnecessary duplication of the pastors' efforts. Both ministers do not have to attend all functions, but their accountability one to another should be made plain to everyone else involved. Above all pastor colleagues must do all they can to make sure they are not seen as competing with one another. Competition from the pulpit is not edifying. Differences in abilities there will inevitably be, but these must be turned into fruitful advantages for increasing the breadth of our Lord's ministry in a locality, rather than grounds for personal rivalry. Here the frankly discussed agreed contract can be of special help. Misunderstandings also arise from differences in age, training, style, and the like. For example, recently trained ministers will inevitably have been caught up in the liturgical revision and development that has taken place in all the denominations. The young minister must be sensitive to the fact that sometimes these developments overturn long-cherished and heart-felt ways of conducting worship. Taking account of your colleague's opinions can only help in understanding some of the hesitations of other worshippers. Taking full account of each other's previous experience and training avoids any sense of your own contribution being under-valued.

One of the most valuable benefits of a close working relationship is the opportunity of being pastors to one another. Where hard choices and difficult counselling are encountered in the pastor's work it is essential that he is able to share the burden. The minister of religion is so often alone when attempting to deal with complex issues involving the well-being and future of individuals and families; perhaps more alone than any of the other caring professionals. The colleague is the person who can draw the sting, share the burden, offer constructive criticism, and be the sounding-board for ideas for progress. This not only increases the effectiveness of the pastor, but also relieves him, and often his family, of the disastrous consequences of carrying such a responsibility quite alone. Surely such support is vital for every pastor.

Another advantage of being pastors together is the opportunity it provides for study and learning. Too often the chance of learning together is jettisoned in favour of what appears more vital business. Not only does study increase our effectiveness as individual pastors, but it may also build our relationship. With a colleague of mine our differences in outlook, which so affected our work, only became evident whilst studying a completely unrelated topic. How glad we were that we had taken that hour for discussion as it opened new possibilities in our work, unhindered by previous misunderstanding. Bible, books and journals are another set of valuable tools for pastor colleagues. Planning, the diary, and business matters should ideally go hand in hand with study together.

In even the best ordered of relationships things are unlikely to go smoothly always. At such times the confidential support and encouragement of an outsider, usually another minister, can play a very significant role. Often all that is required is a listening ear, rather than any direct intervention, but what a relief that listening ear can be! I have been fortunate in being provided with just such outsider in the shape of a post-ordination training tutor. But why are we as ministers so reluctant to provide this kind of support for one another in a less formal way? It is a task which need not take account of denominational boundaries, indeed perceptive contributions from another tradition may be just what is required.

Undoubtedly the most important of all strategies of use in the building of a constructive working relationship is that of regular prayer together. If things have been difficult, tempers frayed, and patience with one another in short supply, commitment to prayer together can often provide the new beginning. Where it is geographically possible the saying together of the Daily Office in a church building is perhaps the best way to maintain that commitment. The reading of scripture, the saying of often repeated psalms and prayers, and the quietness, all provide sufficient formality, solemnity, and objectivity to put personal and working troubles aside. Coupled with this an informal scheme of intercessions for the people the pastors serve, and for each other, ground their efforts together firmly within God's purposes. For those who find the Office too formal these intercessions might provide the basis for their commitment to prayer together.

In an earlier chapter Kenneth Leech wrote of the Eucharist as 'the heart of all Christian prayer, and the source of Christian discipleship' (p. 18). As that is true of all the people of God, so it is of ministerial colleagues. Occasions for sharing the Eucharist are vital. In my own tradition the quiet and meditative celebration of the Lord's Supper in the middle of the week provides a particularly poignant source of renewal for our efforts. Such a service is not meant to detract from Sunday worship but rather to provide an additional and particular focus for our work together. Many lay members, who would be reluctant to join the ministers in the saying of their prayers, will readily take part in such a Communion service and by their contribution ensure that our worship is both truly earthed and heavenward looking.

The final area of special importance to pastor colleagues is that of their families. If the pastors do not function well together this can often reflect itself in the relationship of their families to one another. The clash of loyalties can have unfortunate repercussions in the life of congregations, no matter how hard the pastors themselves strive to hide their differences. Conversely, however, clergy families which most definitely function in very different ways, yet are seen to relate to one another, can do much to improve the morale of church members themselves worried about just how their families should work. The pastors' families, by being closely concerned for one another, can relieve many of the pressures to which clergy families are subjected. The sharing may often be light-hearted and humorous, but none the less significant for that. The creation of special times for celebration and being together is important. The joyous but simple staff dinners of one Methodist circuit I know could be emulated with advantage elsewhere. Pastor colleagues can also help to provide for each of their families privacy and time for themselves. Well planned duty covering by a colleague can provide you with just the space you and your family need.

Pastors working closely together, formally or simply as friends, can alleviate many of the problems this series of articles has dealt with. Such a relationship can provide stimulus, support, fresh ideas, and a breadth of work that will bring many advantages not only for the pastors themselves, but also their congregations and their families. Such a working together, however, needs careful planning and consideration devoted to it if it is to produce its fullest potential.

# The Minister's Finances

GILLIAN M. WEEKS

Bideford

WITH all the recent talk of ministers under stress, how much of it is due to money problems? A lecturer at a theological college has told me of the discontent and unrest among some young ministers' wives. Too many are saying either, 'I wish I'd never married you', or 'Can't you change your job?' Is money part of the problem?

Pressure is on from many directions — from family with their mutters of 'it's a wicked shame' when they sleep in the sides-to-middle sheets, from children when their 'going home' presents at their birthday party are not expensive enough, from friends when you can't compete with their prawns, steaks and after-dinner mints, from the temptations of Marks and Spencer, from your conscience when you see Christian Aid posters or preach on World Poverty. . . . True we have a house, but it does not solve the problem of where we'll live when we retire; true we have education so we should be able to budget, but that education can give us a taste for theatre, opera, travel, books; true we have the interest of our work, but through that work come demands on our money, visitors, transport, begging letters and the pleadings of the inadequates. Wives can be torn between wanting to help with the church and social work and the mundane need to earn some money.

If the parish is poor then some of the social pressures are off. But as one minister working in the East End said to me, 'We are in a missionary situation here. Our family is so different from the majority of those around, it would just not be fair to send the children to the local school. With their accents, their values, their life-style, they would stand out like a missionary's child in a bush school.' Ideally we all agree that both in Africa and in Britain children should attend the same school as those around them — but in practice can you ask your children to suffer for your ideals? Compromise may mean a fee-paying school.

So what to do?

I think it all hinges on those overworked words, 'life-style'. If we consciously or unconsciously grudge not being able to live at the same standard as our brother who is earning £15,000 a year (and doing a lot less work!) we'll never be content. We must remind ourselves that he is probably feeling just the same about his friend who is getting £25,000. Have you ever heard anyone describing themselves as 'rich'? It's a word we use about others but never about ourselves. Our expectations rise with our salary and we never 'get there'.

I'm the wife of a Methodist minister, recently returned from serving overseas for some years. Whilst abroad great care is taken that the stipend is on the same level as in Britain, balancing up cost of living, paying medical expenses and school fees. But whereas in Britain we are among the poorest paid, in the area where we were living we were among the richest. We lived in a 'Dives and Lazarus' situation, eating our meals within view of the poor people, hands outstretched, by the gate. I recommend a few years in that position for getting things into proportion.

But in Britain the situation is no different. The poor are still 'at our gate' although they are only in view through television and other media. We are aware that people live for a year on what we spend on one new dress, yet it's easier to close our eyes to it.

But this is not a missionary article or an Oxfam appeal! I am writing about ministers' financial problems here in Britain and the Editor asked me to be 'severely practical'. Obviously one cannot generalize. We all have our priorities, commitments, resources, interests — but for what it's worth I'll tell you how we manage.

Most important — we budget and we keep accounts. I found it not such a bore as it sounds, once I got into the routine. There's a certain interest and satisfaction in seeing where the money goes, and the accounts save the worry I used to have — the desperate searching through bags and pockets, and cries of 'I'm sure I had more than that'.

In the early days of our marriage we budgeted by the quarter as our stipend came quarterly. I remember there was a big expense each time. In Autumn we bought the coal, in Winter there was Christmas, in Spring our insurance, in Summer our holiday. Once a year we would keep strict accounts for a month and analyse them — otherwise we did not bother. I put money for housekeeping into a Post Office Book every quarter and drew some out each week for food.

But now the pressure is on. Our three children are teenagers and we are trying to keep our son on to finish at boarding school, so the next few years will be our most expensive. We now keep strict accounts all the time and analyse them each month under eight headings: Tithe, Household, Transport, Fuel, Clothing, Entertainment, Sundries, Books and stamps. (The 'Books and stamps' heading is strictly personal. That is where our temptation to overspend lies and we have to keep a check on ourselves!) We aim to live within 90% of my husband's income and keep a reserve for holidays.

Since we returned from abroad I have not been working — or rather the work I do I don't get paid for! I have taught intermittently in primary schools during our twenty years of marriage with a long break when the children were little and breaks when we changed circuit as is the case now. I contend that it is not usually necessary financially for wives to earn money and personally I find so many interesting, fulfilling and useful things to do apart from my job of teaching that I don't always want to. Money is not important unless you are *really* poor and no one in Britain is anywhere near that level. It's a question again of life-style, priorities and temperament. Happily for our family I can teach or not teach. For wives with career ambitions it is not so easy. A change of circuit or parish may mean the wife having to sacrifice the job she enjoys and puts a strain on many a marriage.

But back to our budget. I'll take each of the main headings in turn. First is tithe. We give away 10% of our income and it must come first — not squeezed in if we have any over. We started this about fifteen years ago when we had a stewardship campaign at our church. We calculated how much we had been giving away and were shocked to see how it compared with what we spent on entertainment, on books, on travel. Now each month we see how much we have given and if we have not exceeded the 10% the money goes into a special fund which accumulates until a cheque is sent somewhere. Until we did this we never realized the satisfaction and the peace of mind it would give. Now if I splurge on something extravagant I don't feel quite so guilty. God wants us to enjoy life and we can if our priorities are right. In Malachi 3 we read concerning tithing, 'Put me to the test, says the Lord of hosts, if I will not open the windows of heaven for you and pour down for you an overflowing blessing'. Well ever since we put God to the test and decided to make that 10% a first priority we have received that overflowing blessing. We have never been short of sufficient money and lack of great wealth has never prevented us from doing what we wanted. Also it's great fun deciding where the cheque is going to be sent.

Next item: household. This is where we save money compared with many of our friends. I cut the family's hair. We don't regularly buy cakes, joints of meat, soft drinks, biscuits, tinned fruit, etc. We buy in bulk from wholesale places. We get our protein from liver, eggs, cheese, soya substitute, dried beans, rather than from pork chops and fillet steak. I make things like cakes, ice cream, mayonnaise, chutney. We adapt and substitute as prices change. We never throw food away, except for the occasional rotten fruit; it all goes into the fridge and from there into the next curry!

We try to take only the food we need and finish it even if we don't like it. (Our children, even as toddlers, have always accepted this and when they first went to school meals were shattered by what they saw being thrown away.) Anyone who has ever fasted or who has lived among hungry people cannot but treat food with respect.

But we live on a feast and fast principal. Every so often, at Christmas, birthday or celebration we splash out on a ham, some gooey bad-for-you cakes, a bottle of wine, a joint of meat, and enjoy them all the more. I remember as a child the thrill of a jelly at a party. Now children get no such excitement. Life is so easy. We are all so spoilt.

Last year, whilst living in a country where flour, bread and rice, milk, margarine and maizemeal (the staple food) had been practically unobtainable for a few months, and when the first news of the Karamoja famine was beginning to filter through, I read in the *Methodist Recorder* a letter entitled 'Real Hardship' telling of an old woman in Bristol who was crying in a shop because for the first time in forty years she couldn't buy her weekly joint. We in Britain have been spoilt for so long that we call that poverty. I can sympathize with the old lady being unable to adapt at her age, but poverty — no.

We have always kept an open house. We rarely have a time when visitors are not staying. In Britain it was usually people with problems — alcoholics, ex-prisoners, homeless, inadequates. In Africa it was fellow workers from rural areas and what I called 'See the work' people — relations, friends, church leaders, student volunteers, Oxfam people, etc. We have gone for weeks and even months without a meal on our own as a family. This obviously puts a strain on resources, but any visitor to our house must live at the same standard as we do. No special meals or fuss — and we try to treat all visitors alike whether they are MPs or down-and-outs.

From what I see, it is often on seemingly small things that money gets frittered away. How much some people must spend on meals out, hairdressers, or photography. How much on small expensive shampoos instead of large chain store family size, on extravagantly used kitchen foil, on air fresheners, aerosol cleaners, on make-up, magazines and ice-cream. I'm sure we've all met people who complain they are poor but spend money unthinkingly on all these things.

And what about cheap unadvertized brands? *Which?* magazine has tested things like shampoos, talcs, cosmetics, soaps, and found the cheap ones are often just the same as the expensive except for a different smell. Anyone insisting on brand names is likely to be wasting their money. So let's not be conned. Let's teach our children to laugh at advertising. Let's join the 'joyful resistance movement' which John V. Taylor suggests in his book *Enough is Enough*.

And another thing — Why buy a new pram for your baby when there are so many good second-hand ones available? Why buy new chipboard furniture when second-hand is proper wood, better looking, half the price and you have the fun of the auction room thrown in?

Now transport. On our return to Britain we found this the most shattering item. I had been saying we should not have a car — there are too many cars in Britain, it's ruining the environment, and so on. My big moral stand only lasted for two weeks. We bought a car because we could not afford the bus fares. Until the government does something to improve and lessen the cost of public transport, and control private transport, I think we are stuck with it. We can only do the obvious — walk or bicycle where we can, share cars, cut down on journeys, use the smallest possible car.

Fuel. In the last ten years we've had two winters in the UK and in neither did we have central heating. Coming from the tropics we felt it! We kept one room warm; I put on my fur boots to do the washing up and resorted to jumpers and socks in bed. One night I found my daughter also wearing her woolly hat, scarf and gloves! But we managed.

This winter our manse will have central heating. I hope we will not succumb to the temptation to overheat so that we can wear short sleeves and cotton dresses. Good stewardship is surely to keep the heating down and wear an extra jumper.

We try to economize. Our immersion heater is switched on twice a week for washing clothes and for baths. Any visitor who expects a bath every day can lump it. Water for washing up has been heated in a kettle for the last three years as we've no kitchen water heater. It's a nuisance but I've got used to the routine of switching on the kettle before clearing the table. I try not to use the oven too much, and when I do, I cook lots at the same time. A pressure cooker helps — so do two large thermos flasks into which I pour any hot water left over after making tea, etc.

Clothing. The only new clothes I buy are underwear, stockings and shoes. Everything else comes from 'Nearly New' shops. There are some marvellous ones around. I wonder why anyone buys anywhere else — though I'm glad they do! My favourite London 'Nearly New' shop has a far wider selection of clothes than most London stores. I buy designer clothes, Jaeger suits, etc, for about a third of the new price. They have all been cleaned, cannot have been worn more than a few times and are completely undistinguishable from new.

Jumble sales, if you can stand the indignity of the fight, are a great source of good clothes, of buttons, zips, wool for unpicking, and material for children's clothes if you are willing to unpick amateur dressmakers' disasters. If you go as a helper you can take the first pickings! You have to be ready to poke through piles of smelly rubbish, but you have the excitement of the search and prices are ridiculously cheap.

I know I digress but why in our society do we keep wanting new clothes, feel ashamed of wearing a darned jumper or last year's coat. Is it our image we are trying to protect? Maybe the fashionable lady down the road is compensating because her husband does not love her, just as the man in the flashy sports car may be trying to look big because he is humiliated at work. Christians have their security from God. We shouldn't need ultra-smart clothes, big cars, impressive houses or (dare I whisper it?) a string of degrees, to get our status.

Entertainment. We happen to like ornithology and philately. If your hobby can also be profitable like stamp collecting (or writing articles) so much the better. There are so many cheap or free things to do that it seems pointless to list them. If anyone is bored in Britain today it's the fault of their personality, not lack of opportunity.

For holidays we used to have a caravan. Whilst abroad

we always went camping or exchanged houses. In Britain the exchange of houses seems an obvious solution for many, others like being hosts at holiday homes or travel couriers.

So those are our main budget headings. But however practical and sensible one tries to be, it is one's attitude to finance which is all important.

I've talked about this recently to many ministers and their wives and they were unanimous in their belief that acceptance of lower relative standards must be positive and cheerful. Low pay can be a binding force between ministers' families — only see the wives when they get together — an instant sharing and understanding. Low pay gives ministers a sort of status among their congregations and mitigates feelings that they are parasites on the church. In every debate on ministerial stipends there are many ministers who fight against an increase, and in every series of letters to church newspapers there are many who are ashamed and saddened by those who complain. Low pay prevents a charge of hypocrisy when preaching on economic matters and, most important I believe, it challenges the secular view that the importance of work is displayed by the size of the salary attached.

To finish on a more mundane level with a few 'severely practical' suggestions. Subscribe to, or consult at the library, the consumer magazine *Which?* It has saved us a fortune. Go shopping as little as possible; 'just looking around' is fatal — for me anyway. Buy furniture and household goods in house sales and auctions or from adverts in the local newsagent's window, and keep by your bedside John V. Taylor's *Enough is Enough* — and keep reading it!

# Administration

WILLIAM D. HORTON, M.A.

Sevenoaks

ADMINISTRATION is an important part of any pastor's responsibility. The church is not simply a divinely spiritual entity divorced from the affairs of the world, a soul without a body; it is an organization with a human face and material concerns. As such, its earthly life needs to be 'ordered' and its business conducted efficiently. Where there is good administration God is glorified and his kingdom served; where there is maladministration the body doesn't function properly and God's work is hindered.

Administration is not solely the pastor's responsibility and it is even less that of his long-suffering partner! The church's lay officials have their part to play in the smooth running of the ecclesiastical machine. But the pastor is the key figure. The quality of his leadership determines whether or not the administration serves its purpose; it also determines how effectively others make their contribution. In this, not all pastors are equal. Some have the gift of administration (1 Corinthians 12[28]); finding this aspect of their work both easy and congenial their temptation is to make it the main pre-occupation of their ministry. Others are not naturally business-like and have difficulty with administration; their temptation is to regard themselves as 'above' such a mundane matter and, by neglecting it in favour of more 'spiritual' pursuits, to rejoice in their inefficiency. To yield to either of these temptations is a betrayal of ministry. Every pastor must give necessary administration its proper place (and no more) in his work;

he must neither allow it to become an end in itself, nor must he dismiss it as irrelevant to his calling. His problem is to see it in its true perspective and, then, to fulfil his responsibility to the best of his ability. This article seeks to respond to that two-fold problem both theologically and practically, under the three headings of office, time and personnel management.

## Office management

It is unrealistic to imagine that the pastor's study is simply the place where he reads theology, prepares sermons, prays and is available for pastoral consultation, shut off from outside distractions. In most cases it is also his office where the day-to-day business of the church is transacted and where the telephone, filing and record cabinets, typewriter and other secretarial tools are kept alongside the books and the prie-dieu. This is both biblically and theologically right! The Christian faith is all-embracing; it declares that matter and spirit are equally God's concern and inextricably bound up in the wholeness of human life. God who is Spirit created the material universe, bringing order out of chaos and fashioning all things according to his purposes (Genesis 1 and 2); God who is Spirit became incarnate in Jesus Christ, his Son (John 1). Therefore, to dismiss ordinary, everyday, material concerns as unimportant is unchristian and to contrast the pastor's 'real' work (i.e., his spiritual work), with his administrative duties is to posit a dangerously false dichotomy between the sacred and the secular in life. Maintaining the church fabric, raising money, paying bills, completing schedules and writing letters are no less important facets of the pastor's work than proclaiming the Word, building up the fellowship and ministering to the needy. They service the pastor's work of preaching and caring and are an essential and integral part of the one indivisible ministry of Christ in the church and the world. In fulfilling his administrative duties the pastor is not wasting time which could be more profitably spent in other ways; he is sharing in God's continuing, creative activity and providing the ordered structures through which God's Spirit acts in human life today.

If this is a proper understanding of the place of administration in church life, the practical implications are clear: the work must be done as effectively and efficiently as possible because it is the work of God's kingdom. The best people for the job, the most suitable equipment, and the most appropriate methods must always be employed. The realistic pastor knows that it isn't necessary for him to do everything himself for the church office to function effectively. People in the congregation have secretarial skills and business experience which, in all probability, he has never had and are, therefore, much better able to manage the office than he. Let such people be fully used! If, in a church with a large membership and considerable community involvement, the amount of administration warrants either full or part-time paid secretarial help, the use of church funds for this purpose and the setting aside of church premises for an office are entirely justified. Where the administration is not so demanding there are usually people prepared to give their services as a commitment to Christ; retired business people, young mothers whose family responsibilities prevent them from seeking paid employment, church members who don't feel called to teach in the Sunday School or able to visit the sick, these and many others are often prepared to give their office skills and, in their own time, to make a valuable contribution to the church's administration.

The most suitable equipment for the pastor's administrative work is not necessarily the most sophisticated or costly. The vast majority of churches don't need (even if they could afford) word-processors, memory-typewriters, computers or any of the other electronic marvels used in big business concerns today. Some pastors claim to find great benefit in 'radiopaging', British Telecom's service which enables contact to be made with a subscriber when he is away from his home base, around and about the parish. Others regard an automatic telephone answering device as indispensable for their work. The advantage of being able to answer the telephone twenty-fours a day must be weighed against the disadvantage of using an impersonal machine to do what is best done personally; the pastor must decide for himself whether someone 'phoning him (say) in a moment of acute crisis would be better served by hearing a recorded invitation to speak a message or by hearing the unanswered ringing tone.

Some such items of equipment may be superfluous to the pastor's ministry. But, undoubtedly, others are basic to his work. A large filing cabinet (with a lock and key) in which to store accumulated papers and, even more important, from which to retrieve them readily when they are needed, is essential. A record-card drawer where the register of church members, sermon references and illustrations, indexes of talks and addresses and other important data can be stored is equally necessary. For the mass of printed ephemera which comes the pastor's way and for anything else which need not be preserved a monster wastepaper basket is indispensable! An efficient typewriter is required not only for dealing with official correspondence and committing sermons to paper, but also for cutting stencils if the church's magazine or weekly notice-sheets are 'do-it-yourself' publications. A duplicator (or photo-copier) soon repays its initial cost and the church ought to give its pastor ready access to one. But kindly offers of worn-out machines, off-loaded on to the church as the easiest method of disposal, should be politely but firmly declined! The church's equipment is given hard wear and is operated by many different pairs of hands and it needs, therefore, to be of sound quality, regularly serviced and maintained in first class working order. Nothing is more frustrating to the pastor or destructive of the goodwill of his helpers than a machine which doesn't function properly and causes problems every time it is used. If the end-product is of less than professional standard the church's image is cheapened; only material of the highest quality is worthy of the cause it is meant to serve and, to produce that, the best equipment is essential.

Pastors vary in the way they choose to organize their office responsibilities and every pastor needs to work out a method which is best for himself and his situation. But certain points are of general importance and, therefore, worth noting. It is, for instance, easier to be methodical than unmethodical, not vice versa! Not troubling to file letters received (or to keep copies of those sent) or to replace books on the shelf, causes far more bother later when these things are needed again and a long search has to be made for them. Not dealing promptly with matters requiring attention doesn't, in the long run, save time; it only causes irritation to those kept waiting for the pastor's response. The 'pending' tray should be cleared, the desk tidied and piles of books sorted out at regular and frequent intervals! It is important to keep membership and other church records up-to-date. The pastor ought to be no less efficient (or careful of confidentiality) than the doctor, in recording dates of visits and keeping pastoral notes about his members; should he die suddenly on the job, his successor ought to find everything in order, not in confusion! Financial and legal matters need managing with meticulous care. It isn't often that the pastor is directly responsible for any of the church accounts but, in the course of his work, he frequently handles other people's money. Carelessness can lead to abuse, and the pastor owes it to himself and those who trust him to make a note, at the time, of any money he receives, to issue a receipt, and then to hand on the money to the treasurer of the appropriate fund as soon as possible.

If the pastor's method of working can include something of a personal touch, so much the better. People are more likely to respond favourably to a duplicated or printed letter if it is individually addressed and personally signed; writing the subscriber's name on the church magazine pushed through the letter box, or scribbling a brief note on the visiting card when the member is out are small but important testimonies to the personal nature of Christian ministry and well worth the effort involved. However efficient the pastor's administrative methods may be, if they give the appearance of being coldly impersonal they don't serve the best interests of his work.

### Time management

Time is a valuable, limited, diminishing and non-renewable resource. If, as someone would have us believe, it has no 'before' or 'after' and stands entirely on its own, the wise seize its opportunities to the full; the years slip quickly away and when 'time is up' there is nothing more. But if, as Christians affirm, time has an eternal dimension far beyond the present moment it is even more important to take it seriously. A resource which God has created to reflect the eternal, limitless world of his Spirit, which is an expression on earth of the timelessness of heaven and which he has given mankind as the framework for discovering life's meaning must not be taken for granted, misused or regarded (in contrast with eternity) as unimportant. It is in this context that the pastor, as administrator, exercises time management both for himself and for others.

The pastor's time is the subject of two commonly held, incompatible notions. Some imagine him to have a one-day-a-week job and, once his Sunday commitments are fulfilled, to be a gentleman of leisure. Others assume that his work is so demanding that there are insufficient hours in the day for him to exercise his ministry adequately or to have time for anything else. Neither notion has much basis in reality! The first is held by those (usually outside the church's life) whose ignorance is coloured by Jane Austen's picture of the eighteenth-century country parson with time on his hands and who have no comprehension of the nature and extent of the pastor's responsibilities today. The second gains credence in church circles where a heavy programme of activities demands the pastor's attention and where his members expect him to prove their church's vitality by being constantly busy in 'the Lord's work'. Although to subscribe to either of these notions is a mismanagement of time and a betrayal of stewardship, the pastor's greater temptation is to conform to the latter image. There *are* many time-consuming calls made upon him and he *does* work unsocial hours; some important concerns *do* get crowded out because there are only twenty-four hours in the day. But, it must be admitted, there is often much personal satisfaction to be gained from brandishing a full diary. A pastor who is basically unsure of himself as a person finds his security in always having things to do; one who is uncertain of his role in society may invest his ministry with significance by being hyper-active.

Whatever the reason for it, having insufficient time is as clear an indication of maladministration as having too much.

How then should the pastor seek to manage his time? Primarily by controlling his diary and not allowing it to control him! The most Christian service a pastor can give his people is to live a full, disciplined and unhurried life which reflects the peace of the eternal world in the rush of the temporal. This means giving time to 'being' as well as 'doing'; to keeping still before God as well as being active in his service. It means planning the day's work, but allowing time to contain the emergency when it arises and to respond to the unforeseen demands of people in need. It also means taking sufficient 'time off' for leisure, relaxation and family enjoyment. If, to do these things, the pastor cannot accept every invitation to speak or to be present at every committee meeting, so be it. What can't be delegated must go undone; the kingdom of God is not likely to suffer either serious or permanent damage!

The pastor's administrative responsibilities involve him in the management of other people's time as well as his own. His church members spend most of their daily lives outside the church structures and (those, at least, who take a leadership role) are busy people with professional, family and community commitments. His main task, therefore, is to ensure that the limited time such people have to give to 'church work' is not completely absorbed in servicing the ecclesiastical machine. They must be encouraged to give time to worship, fellowship and building themselves up in the faith so that their Christian witness in the world is adequately sustained. When they are asked to shoulder the important business and material concerns of the church the pastor owes it to them to make sure that time generously given is well spent, that meetings are conducted expeditiously and that their contribution to the work of God's kingdom is properly recognized.

*Personnel management*

The church is a community of people who, in their common life, seek to express their faith and unity in Christ and to make him known in the world. Those who are Christ's Body in each place are called to be a living expression of the gospel, making visible the power of God's Spirit to change human lives and demonstrating the power of God's love to reconcile people of different backgrounds, temperaments and abilities. But the church as a human institution, still has to become what it really is! The imperfect members of Christ have yet to be fashioned into his perfect Body in the world. Much needs to be done before, by God's grace, the church fulfils its calling.

In enabling the church to be the church the pastor has a special leadership responsibility. But his leadership model is not the military commander or the political dictator; it is the servant, the model of Christ whose under-shepherd he is. Therefore, in his management of personnel he leads by ministering to people, working with them, bringing the best out of them, giving full value to each one's contribution and ensuring that a spirit of cooperation flows through the common life. As chairman of church meetings he has opportunities for exercising this kind of leadership. He must resist the temptation to manipulate the meeting so that his view finally prevails, as firmly as he must discourage those who, in undue deference to his office, always look to him to speak the last word in the decision-making process. He must be sensitive to the different points of view present in the meeting and allow each its full expression. If, in the end, a common mind doesn't emerge, it is important for the opposing factions to be contained within the fellowship as a whole. Only then is the corporate nature of the church's fellowship made clear.

In the wider activities of the church, the pastor's responsibility is to use every member's contribution for the good of all. Even in the smallest church there are rich resources of talent. These often remain hidden until the pastor gives opportunity and encouragement for them to be offered in the church's worship and service. Where people are hesitant in offering to do a job, for fear of offending someone who has done it a number of years, the pastor uses all his management skills to suggest that a member's faithfulness is not judged by the fifty years or more he fills a particular position in the church, but by his willingness to train others and hand over his job to them. The fellowship is impoverished if the key positions are jealously guarded by a small minority and everybody's gifts are not used effectively. When friction arises (as it's bound to, sometimes, where people of different ages, temperament and outlook work together) the pastor heals the wounds and builds up the fellowship in mutual understanding. If the church is not to betray the gospel, Christians must be seen to love one another and, in this, the pastor is the catalyst of reconciliation. When administration is seen in this light no part of the pastor's work is of greater importance.

# Part V
# Training and Assessment

# The Pastor and Training

JOHN M. SIMMONDS, B.D.

Sheffield

SIXTEEN years ago, I left college after four years of ministerial training — time spent on Biblical Studies, Greek, Theology, Philosophy, and Church History, with an injection of Methodist theology and history, Psychology, Sociology and Pastoral Studies. Books still stand proudly on my shelves, monuments to college days. Since that time it has been a struggle to keep reading. For many ministers, college books are the last big books we buy, and the last we read; the college course is the last to which we devoted time. Why should this be?

Perhaps we were never emotionally committed to biblical and theological study. Academic courses were necessary, but not inspiring. Our brains were worked, but our emotions were untouched.

Perhaps we came to realize that it's possible to run the church without much theological reflection. Talking most of the time to captive audiences, we rarely expect to answer for our faith.

Perhaps we are so rushed off our feet doing, doing, doing, that the church runs us. We do little more than react to situations, events and people — never subject, always object.

Perhaps we consider theological reflection irrelevant anyway, feeling that the work of students and scholars is too esoteric for practitioners. Or we may feel threatened by new ideas and theories, preferring an ostrich-like stance for our own peace of mind!

Nevertheless it seems fair to say that many ministers abandoned theological reflection when they left college. It may be more accurate to say that they never started! After receiving some kind of briefing, they never began to think for themselves. They covered the ground — a grand tour of Church History and Dogmatics, the Bible and Philosophy — but were not motivated to a personal search for meaning.

Many ministers are isolated and have been for years. They have survived only by going deaf to the conflicting voices inside and around them; sometimes dull and depressed, sometimes cynical and angry. Others have followed other interests, finding their chief satisfaction as marriage counsellors, administrators, school managers, property developers, and so on.

During my ministry, I've been fortunate to meet people who are not satisfied with trite answers to questions and confessional statements from the pulpit: from the bright teenager who challenged my extravagant praise of Charles Wesley's hymns by saying, 'It's all right for you, but I need a dictionary to understand them!', to the retired physicist who stops me after a service and says, 'I enjoyed what you said in the sermon, but tell me more'. Such people made me realize that I had not interpreted my beliefs to myself; my views were borrowed. Often I felt threatened when someone presented a contrary view. It became imperative to engage in continuous reflection — always checking out experience, considering fresh ideas, referring back to the Bible and tradition; and seeking for harmony in one's inner self — a satisfactory relationship between conviction, doctrine, practice and personal meaning.

So much calls out for urgent thought and attention; topics which can only be usefully considered from within the crucible of everyday experience:

— Increasing polarization of theological views and modes of spirituality
— Financial and manpower crises in the church
— The flight into conservatism after the unnerving freedom of the 60s and 70s
— Loneliness in Christian vocation, leading to staleness or repressed anger
— Inability to sustain the traditional pastoral office

all cry out for time to be given by every minister to serious reflection and study, alone and with others.

We need training programmes which take active ministry as their context. Every church spends large sums of money upon initial training, believing that a well-equipped minister will perform better. This is the traditional approach in every professional training institution. But now many educationalists know that the best learning takes place when theory is related to practice, practice to reflection, and reflection to mature judgment. A process which starts with initial training (we hope!) and lasts a life-time, giving ministers time and space to stand back — alone, or in company with others — to engage in analysis, reflection, and reformulation of theological and pastoral theory. So we are looking for training which involves reflection, experiment, sharing at every level of a minister's experience; training done in a variety of contexts — alone, with other ministers, in local churches, residentially, with lay people, on-the-job, and so on. It's important to move away from the present situation where the vast majority of the churches' training resources are put into highly expensive schemes of initial training, so that tired and poorly motivated ministers can be helped to evaluate their work, sort out their battered emotions, and engage in creative theological reflection.

A number of different approaches to further training are possible, each one with strengths and weaknesses, but all valuable:

## 1. *Residential periods*

Many churches pay for ministers to attend residential courses, say from a week to a month's duration, from time to time during their working life. Some courses are arranged by the churches themselves, others by outside agencies. The value of such periods is to allow time and space for a detached view of one's ministry without interruptions — no telephone, no frantic sermon preparation, no acute pastoral needs. Participants commit themselves to an intense programme albeit only for a fortnight or so. Many methods have been used in the training, including experiments in group dynamics and personal encounter, times for silent reflection, activities in creative art and drama, as well as more familiar lectures, seminars, and group discussions. The advantage of such courses is that they guarantee time and space for a great deal to happen. Participants are free to involve themselves fully. Their churches, families, and they themselves recognize that the minister is 'on a course' — free to study and train — an immensely valuable feeling! Such courses facilitate in depth experiences, where people are face to face with others for a considerable time. Such encounters can be deeply disturbing, whilst at the same time invaluable for learning. Without stirred emotions nothing is ever learned. Also, there is value in a course away from familiar people and places. People can speak frankly knowing that they will not have to live for ever with the people on the course. Away from home they can unload themselves in a less inhibited fashion.

Residential courses have limitations. They are expensive to mount and so are often too short and too infrequent. Some potentially good courses have been truncated by tight budgets and participants have been left disorientated, needing the healing which more time and space could have afforded. Another problem is that reflection away from one's regular contacts can be unreal. One can too easily pursue only fantasies, without the checks of a regular situation. Away from home we fall into the trap of talking about people and not with them. In spite of such limitations residential courses can be most valuable, when skilfully led and when the participants are committed.

## 2. Non-residential training

The pattern of non-residential training will be determined by the tasks set and by the expectations of the people involved. Here are a few examples:

(a) Short 'one-off' sessions on topics of current importance. Recent examples are one-day conferences on the Nationality Bill, the ministry of Healing, recent developments in Gospel Criticism, a workshop on Unemployment, and a seminar on the Church of England's Alternative Service Book. The main purpose of such events was to impart information, pool ideas, and talk with experts and others keen on the subject. The value of such events is that they are fairly cheap to run, often with self-catering arrangements, and they demand a small amount of time from the participants. The disadvantage is that they can be too superficial if too much is attempted in too short a time. One day on a topic should not fool us into thinking that we have done it, like a tourist doing the English Lake District in an afternoon!

(*b*) *Long-term courses,* say on a one-day-a-month basis, such as Study Days for Clergy, mounted by university extra-mural departments, or urban ministry courses run by centres like the Urban Theology Unit in Sheffield, England. Topics are valuably covered at a rate at which most hard-pressed ministers can cope, given the motivation; familiar topics like biblical study, theology, contemporary society, liturgy, and so on, updating earlier studies. Ministers can enter new disciplines or develop areas of experience only touched on in initial training, especially areas like counselling, communication, group dynamics, community development, inter-cultural theology, and so on. A valuable contribution made by the Urban Theology Unit is in the area of situation analysis and theological re-formulation, where participants work both in a clergy group and with people in their own neighbourhoods, considering the life of the church and community, the nature of the gospel, engaging in Christian action, and formulating new alternatives for ministry and gospel interpretation. The advantage of such courses is that a minister can take such a programme in his stride, giving time to individual reading and project work between sessions. Valuable relationships can be formed near to home, providing a useful antidote to loneliness and isolation. A disadvantage is that such courses often start well, but often experience a high drop-out rate, as well-intentioned ministers allow undertakers and synods to steal their valuable time!

(*c*) *Group commitments.* One cannot underestimate the value of clergy groups, staff meetings and other valuable training groups. Some groups study books together, others meet regularly to hear one another present a paper, others discuss the lectionary for the next few weeks, others consider articles from a journal to which they all subscribe. All this happens in many cases alongside a programme of ecumenical worship and activity in a particular community. When taken seriously such groups are of great importance, especially when long term relationships are formed. The danger of such gatherings is that sharing stops at a superficial level. To prevent this groups might engage in joint activity — more than mere talk.

(d) *Engagement with other disciplines.* Every town or city offers a wide range of opportunity for training — some closely related to the work of the pastor, some unrelated — but all giving important openings for the sensitive minister to develop self-awareness and appreciation of others and the environment: e.g. joining a course for Religious Education teachers, training with a group of marriage guidance counsellors, attending local evening classes, forming a regular seminar for community workers in an area. Listening to people of other disciplines is invaluable, but care must be taken so that such engagements do not crowd out essential theological and personal reflection.

(e) Nothing can replace *training in the local Christian community* in which the minister participates not only as guru but also as disciple. Enormous possibilities for growth are presented when people in a locality work through their hopes and fears, their faith and doubt, the successes and failures. Without reflection in the situation where the action is, so many other valuable courses can be pure escapism, with people going on courses because they cannot see light where they are. Such training calls for a new look at the pastor in his role. If he is seen by others and by himself only as the one engaged to do good to others, then training will only be partial. But if the pastor learns from and with his fellows, significant growth will take place.

(f) *Training through dialogue and friendship.* An important and unique kind of training takes place when two
people commit themselves to each other in regular sharing,
either as equal partners or as director and directed. Alex
Vidler and Malcolm Muggeridge's relationship is of such a
kind. Secrets are shared, trust is established, friendship
holds through controversy and agreement. Each takes
delight in the other. Genuine listening and talking can take
place. It behoves every minister to find someone who will
listen and talk, honestly, frankly, and lovingly.

The content of all training exercises will be determined by
the needs and interests of the participants. People will be
more committed if they are interested in the course content.
Possibilities are without number: from keeping up-to-date
with theological thought and literature to learning in
encounter groups or by simulation exercises. Every kind of
study should be related to a person's search for meaning — for the self, the group, the community, the church.

Training opportunities are only limited by the imagination and the will of the pastors and their churches.
Denominations must set aside more money for in-service
training, not only to pay for centrally mounted courses, but
also to grant-aid ministers who want to persue an individual
interest. So important is in-service training, reflection upon
and from within ministry, that it may be necessary to
shorten the time given to highly expensive initial training,
which often fails to motivate students into a life-long
programme of study and reflection.

In the end, however, any provision will not motivate
individual pastors, for if anything is to be learned it must be
motivated by personal desire. Such commitment is not
unlike discipleship — being an apprentice, moving in with
the Master Craftsman, working with him and other

apprentices, producing the goods, earning both praise and rebuke; all the time growing in maturity, discovering new resources, and more fully appreciating the task. We are called to be disciples — nothing more, nothing less. Such an expectation should be recognized by the whole church from the day of baptism, and renewed at confirmation and ordination. The churches must release resources so that this expectation can be fulfilled.

# Assessment of Ministry

WILLIAM D. HORTON, M.A.

Sevenoaks

No ONE becomes a pastor by accident or drifts, unchallenged into the Christian ministry. Ministers in the main denominations are ordained only after they have undergone a process of selection, training, examination and probationary service, all designed to test their vocation, assess their suitability for ministry and equip them adequately for their future work. The smaller, independent churches, though less formal in their assessment methods, are equally concerned to ensure that their pastors are truly called of God and fit people to minister to the local congregation. So it is generally recognized that a pastor needs to be a person of evident Christian faith and experience, and one who possesses clearly defined leadership and professional skills. Careful assessment is made of everyone who seeks to become a Christian pastor.

Because of this, it is somewhat strange that little or no regular assessment is made of a pastor's ministry *after* his acceptance by the church. It seems a common assumption that once a person has been ordained, given a 'living' or placed on the 'approved list' of ministers (however the state of initial attainment is described!) every pastor is able to exercise a successful ministry until retirement, without any further assessment of his work being either desirable or necessary. It appears to be taken for granted that his preaching will be fruitful, that his pastoral work will build up the church, that he will be an efficient administrator, and that, as a matter of course, he will always be master of every situation. Unless he is openly immoral, or convicted in a criminal court, his ministry is unlikely to be called in question or his effectiveness as a pastor challenged.

Only when the pastor changes appointment is an assessment (of sorts) attempted. And, then, only when a 'key' appointment in the church is at stake is it likely to be conducted with any degree of professionalism. In the case of most ordinary pastoral appointments the enquiries made about a pastor tend to be superficial rather than of any depth, subjective rather than objective and on the level of 'Do you think J--- S--- will fit in at St Marks?' 'Yes, you'll like him, he's a good chap!' If the pastor has a weaker side to his ministry (and what pastor hasn't?) this tends to be minimized out of mistaken kindness to him and in order not to damage his prospects. Even when the assessment is carried out conscientiously it is unusual for the pastor to be given details of it. He is, therefore, denied any opportunity of profiting from it and using it to shape his future ministry. And if he changes appointments infrequently even this kind of assessment isn't made often.

The lack of any regular assessment of ministry affects both the church and the pastor. No right-minded church allows its central heating system to deteriorate through failure to renew the annual service contract; no church, fortunate enough to have financial reserves, invests them haphazardly; no live, worshipping community omits to review its work periodically in response to changing circumstances. Yet, how rarely is a church concerned to get the best from its most valuable (and most expensive) investment, its manpower! Greater care needs to be taken in handling this resource than in fully utilizing the church's other resources, for more is at stake; whether the pastor is over or under-employed, rightly or wrongly employed ought to come higher on the church council's agenda than even such a major item, say, as the reroofing of the building. The church which fails to maintain, service and assess the work of its pastor fails in a vital area of its stewardship and is bound to suffer long-term consequences.

The pastor, too, suffers from never facing a realistic assessment of his ministry. Because the nature of his calling means that, often he *has* to stand alone, the pastor who *wishes* to isolate himself from the guidance and help of others is able to do so unhindered. Personal and family problems can be concealed successfully from church members. Problems in ministry can arise without anyone (sometimes without even the pastor himself) being aware that they are there or that they are serious. One pastor may die prematurely through overwork because no one has shown him how to delegate his responsibilities or told him that the kingdom of God is unlikely to collapse if he takes a day off! Another may enjoy a leisurely existence and never be fully 'stretched', or may busy himself doing things for which he wasn't ordained while important pastoral duties are neglected, simply because he's never been challenged to examine how he spends his time. Many pastors would not have reached the crisis point of resignation from the ministry if their work had been regularly assessed and they had been helped to come to terms with themselves and their situation. Many others would have been saved from the nagging dissatisfaction and sense of unease which have dogged their continuing service of the church.

Why, then, has the church been so slow to recognize the importance of ministerial assessment and the need for in-service evaluation common in other professions? This article discusses that question and then lists the aims which ought to lie behind an assessment; it concludes by suggesting practical ways in which regular assessments may be carried out.

The root cause of the church's reluctance to introduce any assessment of its pastors may be that, historically, the church has regarded itself as distinct from other institutions in society, operating under different rules and for different purposes; the church is 'holy', its pastors, who are people of vocation, are set apart for *God's* work and specialists in *their* sphere of things spiritual, and to apply to them the personnel procedures used in industry, the civil service and other walks of life is unnecessary and out of place. Often, both pastor and congregation accept this notion too readily! The pastor claims he is accountable to God alone for his ministry and for how he fulfils it. The church member who respects his pastor as a man of God and holds that ordination confers on him all the gifts and graces necessary for his life's work hesitates to ask questions about matters (he considers) outside the layman's province. So, in many parts of today's church there is an in-built, traditional resistance to the idea of assessment of ministry; being unbusinesslike is regarded as a virtue, not a vice!

A pastor may resist an assessment of his ministry for reasons other than that he feels his vocation ought not to be subject to such a procedure. If his training instilled into his mind the belief that he was being fully equipped to deal with the demands of any situation he would be likely to face during his ministry it isn't surprising that, when experience proves otherwise, guilt feelings take hold of him. Provided that he can keep to himself the knowledge that he isn't always able to cope, that he has weaknesses, and that he's not altogether the model pastor his congregation imagines, then he can live with his guilt and frustration. But once the idea of assessment is mooted he immediately feels threatened and becomes defensive. Any enquiry, he suspects, would increase his sense of guilt, reveal his failures to colleagues and superiors (on whom he depends for preferment?) and undermine the respect which his church members give to him and which he needs to justify his calling and boost his morale. But, perhaps, the hardest thing for any pastor to accept is the reality that he is not self-sufficient. Spending his life helping others and being the assessor of *their* situation, he finds it hard to accept help for himself, to share his problems with others and to subject his ministry to open and honest assessment.

However, the entire blame for the lack of assessment mustn't be laid on the pastor's shoulders! There are difficulties in the nature of ministry itself. How can matters which are essentially spiritual be assessed by using other than spiritual criteria? Diagnostic tests can quickly assess the efficiency of an internal combustion engine and an athlete's progress can be measured against the stop watch or metre rule. But how can a pastor's performance be measured adequately? By the growth or decline in church membership during his pastorate? This is likely to be determined as much by sociological as by religious and spiritual factors. By the number and variety of the church activities he has introduced? These may be only of marginal importance in the growth of the church's inner, spiritual life. By the fullness of his diary and the number of hours he gives each week to his job? There is no guarantee that constant activity is a sign of a well-balanced ministry; it may equally be evidence of inefficiency, bad management and a careless use of time. And how can a pastor's priestly ministry of prayer be assessed? Or his care of the needy? Or his power in preaching? The difficulties involved in making any assessment have often been used as arguments for making no assessment at all!

One further problem needs to be mentioned. Very rarely is there a written job description of any ordinary pastoral appointment in the church. It is assumed that everyone knows what a minister does and what the job requires of him. But do they? Different situations call for different qualities in a pastor: the person skilled in inner-city work may not be equal to the demands of an appointment in the country, the university, the armed forces, the suburb or some other area of ministry. In the wide variety of appointments no standard job description is possible and, therefore, no recognized norm against which the pastor's ministry can be assessed. Until there is a full, written job description for every appointment it is difficult to determine the extent to which the pastor matches up to its demands.

If the difficulties can be overcome and the principle of regularly assessing a pastor's ministry find acceptance, what should be the aims of the assessment? The primary object must be to help the pastor rather than to judge him; to enable him to know (and accept) himself, to develop as a person and to replenish his own inner resources; to give him insights into the strengths and weaknesses of his ministry that he can use to make his future work more satisfying and effective; to encourage him to share with others the problems and opportunities of his situation so that he is helped to bear the stresses of the former and seize the challenges of the latter; to open his mind to new ideas, new methods and new areas of service so that he is never entirely bound by the heavy hand of custom and tradition. These are some of the broad aims which ought to lie behind any assessment of ministry. Only a positive and forward looking evaluation will help the pastor.

How can an assessment with these aims be put into practice? Four methods (not mutually exclusive) immediately come to mind: self-assessment, assessment by the congregation, peer assessment and external (professional?) assessment. Each has its advantages and drawbacks but any one of them would bring benefit to a pastor willing to cooperate in working it through.

1. *Self-assessment*. This method is perhaps the most rewarding but, unquestionably, it's also the most difficult and demanding. Truth which a person discovers for himself has deeper and longer-lasting influence on his thinking than truth demonstrated to him by somebody else. And, because self-assessment can be incorporated into the pastor's regular pattern of life it doesn't suffer from being regarded as an imposition made upon him (always at an inconvenient time!). But honesty and discipline are essential! Pretence comes as easily to the unwary pastor as to anybody else, and 'turning the blind eye' can often be his unconscious reaction to negative and adverse factors. No useful purpose is served by attempting to *prove* anything, whether it be one's own sanctity and success, or miserable sinfulness and failure. Again, like most other people, most pastors live and work between the two extremes and, however difficult it may be to practise, the Delphic precept 'know thyself' must be the self-assessor's rule. Self-discipline is necessary if the pastor is to avoid casualness on the one hand and over-intensity, leading to unhealthy introspection, on the other.

If the pastor decides to follow the self-assessment method there are various actions he can take. He can adopt a 'rule' of life by which he regularly measures his vocation. He can prayerfully review each day's events at the day's end. Every few months, for a day or longer, he can make his 'retreat' to reflect on the effectiveness of his ministry. Every year, on the anniversary of his ordination he can write down his hopes (realistic ones!) so that twelve months later he can assess achievement in the light of intention. The way of self-assessment is open to all, but none finds the going easy!

2. *Congregational assessment*. This method is also fraught with problems, but pastors who have used it testify

to its value. It is essential for both pastor and people to show charity and goodwill, particularly if the congregation is one of those which has considerable say in the hiring and firing of its ministers! The representatives of the congregation appointed to carry out the assessment need to have a proper understanding of the nature and scope of the pastor's work, both within and outside the church structures. They must look neither for a superman to whom they can safely entrust the success of their church, nor for a scapegoat on whom they can blame their own failure. But given qualified laymen prepared to undertake it, this congregational assessment has two main advantages: it is carried out by people familiar with the local situation and it provides the opportunity for pastor and people, together, to evaluate the ministry of their church and not simply that of their pastor. What is the church achieving? What progress is being made in its life of worship, fellowship, evangelism and Christian Service? What are its plans for the future and how does it propose to implement them? Answering these questions assesses the church's work and, within that context, the pastor's leadership role is evaluated as well.

3. *Peer assessment.* The pastor who belongs to a team ministry, or who shares colleagueship with others in a regular staff meeting, has considerable advantages over the pastor who works on his own. He has a ready-made peer group in which corporate evaluations of ministry can be made as a matter of normal practice. The team members may work in the same situation, but they bring to the shared task differences of approach, a variety of insights, and a diversity of gifts, all of which challenge the individual pastor to reassess his own ministry against the contributions of others. To some extent this happens automatically, but assessment of ministry ought to be one of the team's

declared aims rather than a by-product of its staff meetings. Time and effort should be spent in evaluating the part each pastor plays; a trustful atmosphere needs to be created in which each team member is able to react to the others, to make criticisms without giving or taking offence, and to offer challenge, encouragement and support to the group. A pastor who works on his own and is, therefore, denied this method of assessment can benefit from it in a limited way if he seeks out one or two neighbouring pastors who are similarly placed and who would be willing to share in a mutual evaluation of their ministries.

4. *External assessment.* If objectivity is rated as an important factor in any assessment, this method offers the best hope of obtaining it. Someone from outside can assess a situation more clearly than a person intimately involved in it. The responsibilities of the *pastor pastorum*, whether bishop, moderator or district chairman ought to include the appointment of an assessor for every pastor in his care (indeed, those responsibilities ought to include undertaking the assessment of his pastors himself, *ex officio!* But the numbers involved and the many other demands made on him preclude him giving any individual sufficient time and attention to do the job properly, even if he is suitably qualified). He may appoint someone after the model of a spiritual director with whom the pastor can meet regularly to discuss, in confidence, every aspect of his ministry. He may introduce the pastor to one of the Christian organizations specializing in professional assessment techniques and ensure that the church authorities pay the consultation fees incurred. Or he may encourage the pastor to use one of the residential centres which provide opportunities for further training, for 'retreat' and for courses which contain an element of assessment. Whatever form it takes, it is sensible for an external assessment of a pastor's ministry to

be carried out at least every five years. And it is important that it include a medical check-up; the pastor's effectiveness at work is not unrelated to his physical and mental health!

At present, few pastors undergo any form of regular assessment during the course of their ministry; there is a long way to go before even the principle of such evaluations is generally accepted, by pastors and the church as a whole. None the less, attempts are being made to initiate schemes and there are stirrings of support in the councils of the different denominations. These may be clouds no bigger than a man's hand, but they foreshadow the day when as much care will be given to assessments after a person becomes a pastor as is now given to evaluating him before his acceptance.

# The Contributors

The Reverend Canon Norman Autton is Chaplain at the University Hospital of Wales, Cardiff.

The Reverend James B. Bates is Chaplain at Southlands College, Wimbledon, a Constituent College of the Roehampton Institute of Higher Education.

The Reverend J. David Bridge is a Secretary of the Home Mission Division of the Methodist Church.

The Reverend Christopher P. Burkett is Team Vicar of St Luke's in the Leek Team Ministry, Staffordshire.

The Reverend Geoffrey L. Clark is a Methodist Minister at Cheadle Hulme and Superintendent of the Bramhall Circuit.

The Reverend Bruce Grainger is Vicar of St John Baildon with St James and St Hugh, West Yorkshire, Chairman of the Bradford Diocesan Liturgy and Music Group and a member of the General Synod of the Church of England.

The Reverend William D. Horton is a Methodist Minister, Superintendent of the Sevenoaks Circuit, Kent, and Connexional Candidates' Secretary.

The Reverend Dr Edmund S. P. Jones, formerly Minister at the Queen's Cross Church, Aberdeen, is now Minister of the New York Avenue Presbyterian Church in Washington, D.C.

The Reverend Kenneth Leech is Race Relations Field Officer of the Board for Social Responsibility of the General Synod of the Church of England.

The Reverend Dr Henry McKeating is a Methodist Minister and a Senior Lecturer in Theology at the University of Nottingham.

The Reverend Dr Graham A. Patrick is a Methodist Minister at Alsager, Cheshire.

The Reverend John M. Simmonds is a Methodist Minister in Sheffield, actively involved in in-service training.

The Reverend Dr Kenneth Stevenson is Anglican Chaplain to the University of Manchester and has written *Family Services* (SPCK, 1981).

Mrs Gillian M. Weeks is the wife of a Methodist Minister. She describes her experiences in *Married to a Minister* (Epworth Press, 1980) under the pseudonym Gillian Simonson.